Fearless Public Speaking

How to Destroy Anxiety, Captivate Instantly, and Be Memorable.

Always Get Standing Ovations

By Patrick King, Social Interaction Specialist
at www.PatrickKingConsulting.com

Table of Contents

Introduction

I was sweating bullets.

I made a bad joke, didn't commit to it, and apologized for it. Three cardinal sins within the first minute.

No one in the audience so much as gave me a pity laugh, and the only thing I could hear was my heart beating wildly in my chest.

Public speaking and presenting were never my strong points when I was younger, and it was never more apparent than during that report about owls in grade school. I made the mistake of believing that I could wing it, which meant that my eyes were glued to my notes... which were becoming increasingly difficult to read because my hands were fluttering like birds.

Every time I looked up from my notes and inadvertently made eye contact with one of my bored audience members, it was a shock to my fight or flight impulse and I became even more aware that I was bombing.

After I finished my presentation, I excused myself to the restroom where I proceeded to mop myself dry of the nervous sweat I had produced.

It was a feeling of helplessness that I hated. I wasn't a particularly shy child, but whenever I got in front of a crowd, I froze and started acting like someone completely different.

This trend followed me until the beginning years of college where I actually made note of my self-destructive patterns and was proactive about changing them. Public speaking and presenting was an area where I made a concentrated effort to improve, and the first question I asked myself was "Who can I watch and copy?" Generally a good rule of thumb for novices in any field.

It only took me a second to realize I wouldn't have to look very hard for the best speakers because they were right in front of my face – standup comics.

When you think about it, standup comics are amazing speakers. There are two main reasons for this: (1) their standard of success; and (2) they expect negative feedback.

First, for a standup comic to consider a performance a success, they have to be making people laugh, on command, for an hour at a time. It's not just going up there and not messing up, or being mildly charming. Success to them is a laugh riot. Objectively, that must rank as one of the most difficult things to do in the world when you factor in the vast differences in senses of humor that exist. Our definition of a successful performance would be pitiful to a standup comic.

Second, standup comics essentially go to war when they perform. If they don't do well, their audience will let them know by booing, hissing, and heckling, all of which are welcomed. They constantly have to deal with hostile crowds and are in the business of winning them over. It's a scary thought, and a far cry from the consequences the rest of us face if we bomb a performance – we only have to cope with varying degrees of feeling awkward.

With hours of watching standup comics perform under my belt, I was able to approach my next presentations with a bit more confidence and aplomb.

This book encompasses the difficult lessons I've learned, and the forays outside my comfort zone I've taken to increase my public speaking and presentation skills so that I can captivate others and be a memorable speaker. Like most of our skills, speaking prowess is easily improvable. You just need a proven compass and a willingness to explore and shipwreck.

The amount of crashing and burning I suffered through – at Toastmasters and other similar organizations – is impressive and extensive. But my world didn't end, my face didn't melt from embarrassment, and my friends didn't shun me because I flubbed a speech or made a joke that no one laughed at.

That's the funny thing about public speaking – even though you're on the stage and the focal point for the audience, they don't care that much about what you do. They won't remember your missed jokes or fumbled words. It's easier to walk onto a ledge that might crumble if no one is looking, so let this book be the blindfold you need to become an amazing speaker.

Chapter 1. Overcome Anxiety and Stage Fright

Chances are you have some long-held preconceptions about speaking in front of others.

First, you may have told yourself that you're bad at it. To that I reply that you are, and will be, if you *think* you are.

Second, you've probably told yourself that it's a scary proposition. Standing up in front of a group of people and speaking is one of the things people fear most in life, and it's been confirmed by innumerable studies. You're putting yourself in a position where you are vulnerable to judgment – of course that's daunting, especially if your baseline of self-confidence isn't spectacularly high.

This fixation on judgment becomes a self-perpetuating cycle that makes you perform even more poorly. When you feel anxiety behind an action, you become self-conscious and start to walk on eggshells because of the literal and figurative spotlight. The more anxious you become, the more fear festers inside you. Even for the best speakers in the world, sometimes it's difficult to shake off the feeling of impending doom at the thought of this worst-case scenario.

All the humor, wit, and preparation you put into presenting can be flushed down the toilet if you let your anxiety and fears get the best of you. When you get into this state of mind, you inevitably magnify every single little stumble or stutter you make, all the while downplaying the overall skill and ease with which you might have presented.

The second you have one poor presentation, you might feel that you're "bad at speaking." But imagine if we made our judgments for everything else based on one occasion that happened twenty years ago? That show-and-tell segment in third grade is long gone, so it's time to overcome the subconscious damage that was dealt. Realizing the irrationality of our fears is often what gets us through them. I like to think that this book is a tremendous step forward in that direction.

The first step to defeat your fear of presenting and speaking is to *adjust your perspective.* The way you perceive your role, the role of the people in the audience, and the context has a tremendous effect on how comfortable you are with it.

It's really all about how you choose to view a particular situation. Are you going out there to be judged by a crowd of strangers foaming at the mouth to pick you apart? Well... most likely not.

Let's take a common example from dating.

When we are around people we desire, we feel self-conscious and judged because we aren't sure if we are good enough for them. But put us in front of someone we don't desire, and suddenly words fall freely from our mouths because we aren't afraid of judgment. How we feel about our audience dramatically changes our approach.

The reality is that the audience is there to see *you*. You are at least part of the reason they decided to skip work, take a weekend, or just take their lunch hour to hear you speak. In 99% of these situations, you are indeed desirable and pursued in the same vein that someone is pursuing you romantically. They are there for you. They want to learn from

11

you. They have sacrificed something to see you. They are there to cheer you on and they actually want you to succeed.

Whether you are the main event, the undercard, the space-filler, the teacher, or professor, people are your captive audience. They want something from you, and that by itself puts you in a position of desirability. This is a much different perspective than thinking you are a lamb being led onto the stage for slaughter.

And what if they don't want anything to do with you? Now that's a tough challenge. Take this chance to make them change their minds about you! How many people can you win over, and how quickly?

If you're put into a situation you aren't particularly comfortable in, the only choice you have is to modulate your emotional response and perspective. You can choose to dig yourself further into that hole created by anxiety and fear, or you can realize your inherent value just by being in front of people that are there to see you.

Once you can embody this sense of comfort – instead of anxiety – the next level is to realize that your audience, whoever it might be composed of, isn't looking for perfection.

The more human you are, the easier it is for people to connect with you, as long as you are above a certain threshold of performance – in other words, you're not absolutely terrible.

In fact, there's an entire psychological phenomenon called the Pratfall Effect that essentially says that the more vulnerable you appear, the more likable you are. Stumbling, stuttering, making a mistake with your visuals, and self-deprecating jokes – as long as they don't signal underlying incompetency – are errors that actually increase your charisma and likability.

Instead of being afraid of your vulnerabilities and your shortcomings, embrace them. They communicate unequivocally that you are human just like they are. The more connected they feel, the easier it is for them to identify with you.

Your audience doesn't just become personally connected; they are emotionally connected from the second you step onto your stage. In other words, whatever you are feeling will instantly transfer to them.

For example, some overweight people are sensitive about their weight; others are not. When we're around those who are sensitive about their weight, we feel as if we have to walk on eggshells and be careful not to insult them because we see they are outwardly uncomfortable. We have to be mindful and think twice about what we say. The result is we act unnaturally.

This is how an audience feels with a speaker who is obviously uncomfortable about being there. Tension is never something you want to feel as an audience member unless it's intentional for effect and you know it will end soon.

Consequently, it's damaging and uncomfortable to tell the audience that you are nervous, tired, or unprepared. You may do this by instinct to lower expectations, or it might simply be true. *But don't tell them*.

Doing so just creates a negative mental instruction: this person is definitely not going to do well. And it colors how you are interpreted. If you tell people you are nervous, they will see everything you do as a negative, nervous tic. Don't put yourself in that ballpark voluntarily.

Along with not telling people you are nervous or tired, don't apologize during or for your performance. Again, the only thing you are accomplishing by apologizing is setting negative expectations in the minds of your listeners. Talk about starting things off on the wrong foot!

To make matters worse, your body reacts physiologically to your psychological stress. When you are anxious or stressed out about a performance (or anything, really) your body releases a hormone called cortisol. Cortisol makes you physically and mentally jittery. Caffeine boosts cortisol production, so don't take caffeine in the hours before a performance.

On the other hand, based on the Yerkes-Dodson Law, you don't want to alleviate 100% of the stress and pressure you feel. According to this model, there is an optimal level of stress that corresponds directly to peak performance.

If you think about real-life examples, this makes perfect sense. When you don't feel any stress about something, such as an exam, you don't study and you don't perform well because you don't think critically about it. It's a lazy state of mind. But when you feel too much stress about something, like an exam that will determine the rest of your life, you might feel too stressed and overwhelmed about the consequences to focus properly on the task at hand.

The Yerkes-Dodson Principle is all about finding optimal levels of pressure so you can perform optimally. Getting the right mix of stress and pressure is tricky. You should focus on being sufficiently motivated to work hard enough to get your mental gears churning, but not allow yourself to get so overloaded that you essentially begin to struggle.

People who are able to operate consistently on a peak level of performance when it comes to speaking in front of a crowd or performing in front of audiences enter a state of flow.

Unfortunately, when you put too little or too much stress on yourself, flow is not triggered. Too little, and you approach something in a sloppy and unmotivated manner. Too much, and you panic.

The secret to Yerkes-Dodson Law is to constantly experiment on your own time and at your own pace regarding the right level of stress and pressure. Trigger these at the right times so you can operate at peak performance.

Just keep in mind that ultimately, the consequences you face for performing or speaking poorly aren't that bad.

Nine times out of ten, the worst consequence is that you'll feel awkward. And people get over awkward. The sun will still rise tomorrow, and people will quickly find new things to latch onto. People will forget. Your career won't die, your significant other won't leave you, and you won't be shunned by society – those things only happen in your head. That's not so bad, is it?

Chapter 2. Nailing Your Opener

If you've ever researched public speaking tips, undoubtedly the first piece of advice you've come across is that your opener is the most important part of your speech. If nothing else, your opener should be entertaining and captivating, such that the rest of your material may not even matter.

This advice isn't wrong, but rarely are you told why it matters and how to do it. The reason you want to craft a compelling opening is twofold.

First, scientists have long known that people's memory tends to fixate on two points in time – the beginning of something, and the ending of something. Presumably, this is because the beginning sets the overall tone, and the ending is the most recent part in terms of time. This is called the primacy (the first aspect) and the recency (the last and most recent aspect) effect. This means that the vast majority of time, people will remember your first and last words more than they will remember what you said in the middle of your presentation.

Second, first impressions matter. When you meet someone at a party or networking event, you might have about sixty seconds to make a first impression. You think that's quick? When you're on stage or in front of people, you have about half that time, and often before you even say anything. You don't have to be perfectly polished or charming, but people will make a decision about your credibility, trustworthiness, and competence very quickly. People don't have the luxury of time when it comes to making decisions about you, so they'll latch onto the first signs they see to judge you.

That's the nutshell version of why you must nail your opener. So how do you actually do it?

On most speaking occasions, you will be introduced by someone who is either organizing the event or presenting before you. Often, you will submit a biography for them to read so people will know relevant points about you.

This is part of your opener! In many instances, this is space you can use to build buzz before you even get onto the stage. Don't squander it, and don't treat it as a nuisance that you have to write. It is part of your presentation and you should treat it as such.

Operative adjectives for your biography should be short, catchy, relatable, interesting, impressive, and humanizing.

At the very least, your biography should be more than the standard resume of where you've worked and all the dry accomplishments you've achieved in your line of work. As important, present everything in a humorous light or emphasize an interesting tidbit in your biography that you can later refer to when you walk on stage. If you can make them smile before you hit the stage, you've won.

Here is a simple structure you can use to create your compelling biographical introduction.

- Two sentences about your work – why are you speaking and why are you relevant?
- One sentence about your background and credentials – why should people listen to you?

- One sentence about your personal life – what makes you interesting and unique as a person? (This part can be tweaked to fit the context in which you're speaking.)

Here's an example where I am speaking at a conference about using small talk skills to increase sales:

Next up, we have Patrick King. Patrick King is a Social Interaction Specialist based in San Francisco, California. He works with clients on a wide range of skills like charisma, conversation, and confidence, and conducts workshops on these same topics. He's a trained lawyer, an international bestselling author, and has been coaching in some form or another for almost a decade. In his free time, he enjoys watching *Shark Tank* to become more vicious, and fronts an 80s cover band. *Don't Stop Believin'* is his favorite song to cover.

The end of that biography also highlights another important point about your opener and presentation in general – keep it light-hearted and try to be relatable as a human instead of just a figure on the stage.

Resist the temptation to pack your whole resume into your opener. It's going to result in information overload which will make people tune out before they even see you.

When you reach the stage, ignore the crowd until they are ready for you. Take a few moments to settle in, adjust the environment to your liking (adjust the microphone stand, pour yourself a glass of water, move the podium, shuffle your notes, clean your glasses, and so on). Resist the urge to engage immediately. Wait for them to grow quiet in expectation. Anticipation will build and you will have a captive audience.

Whichever method you use as an opener (and I've listed a few below with examples), it's important that you speak in terms that make your audience care.

There's no perfect line or method, but the most consistently effective way to open is to appeal to their desires and answer the question, "Why do I care about this speaker and this topic?"

How can you make what you have to say relate to them in a visceral way?

The Shocking Statistic

You can open with a statistic, and the more shocking, interesting, or unbelievable, the better.

For example, at a recent TED talk Jane Fonda said, "There have been many revolutions over the last century, but perhaps none as significant as the longevity revolution. We are living on average today thirty-four years longer than our great grandparents did. Think about that: that's an entire second adult lifetime that's been added to our lifespan."

This is a very powerful intro because she could have focused on the raw statistic, but what did she do? She made it personal. She related it to the audience members' great grandparents and she also addressed the audience members themselves. It has a direct impact on their lifespan, and it's a novel way to view it.

The not-so-engaging way to have done this would have been, "We are now living thirty-four years longer than people who lived 150 years ago. Big deal, right? It's just a number." There is a big difference in how you personalize these statistics and make them relevant to your audience.

Tell a Personal Story

One of the best personal story openers you'll find is Steve Jobs's commencement address at Stanford University in 2005.

He began with the following, "Truth be told, I never graduated from college, and this is the closest I've ever gotten to a college graduation. Today I want to tell you three stories from my life. That's it. No big deal, just three stories. The first story is about connecting the dots. I dropped out of Reed College after the first six months, but then stayed around as a drop-in for another eighteen months or so before I really quit. So why did I drop out? It started before I was born."

This is very powerful opener because by telling a really personal story, he draws people into his world and makes them feel the emotions he felt. It's a glimpse into drama and is essentially a mini soap opera, and we all know how addicting and engaging those are.

When you use a personal story, you just have to make sure it applies to the situation at hand – and that it is short and to the point. Make sure you talk about the emotions involved, and try to be relatable. Finally, if you aren't funny, don't try to make it funny. Stick to your strengths.

The bad way to do a personal story opener is to ramble on about stories about your life that you think are funny but have no relation to the topic at hand. This is extremely self-indulgent and borderline rude; it's a selfish pursuit that your audience may not care about.

Ask a Rhetorical Question

Rhetorical questions are great because they get people thinking quickly. It's an amazing method to engage people; it's easy, direct, and all you have to do is make sure the question is relatable and not abstract.

For example, you might ask, "I'd like to begin by asking you to think about your typical weekday morning routine (pause). Try to picture what it would be like not to rush around on five and half hours of sleep every morning and enjoy a leisurely weekday morning routine instead (pause). Today I'm going to offer you three strategies for making the impossible possible."

When you ask the rhetorical question, you immediately engage them because it's something they can answer personally, and you make it sound as if they need to reevaluate it – so they do so immediately. You give people a chance to visualize an alternative reality. Use the alternative reality as an opening for the points you will cover. This is a very powerful way to quickly get your audience on the same page as you.

Ask a Direct Question

You can ask the audience a question and have them answer it. This is the opposite of a rhetorical question. This directly connects you with them, and makes you appear spontaneous and curious.

However, when you ask a question, you must make sure that you get your desired response from the audience within the first two answers.

For example, if you ask an audience "What do you think of when I say dog?" the audience will very likely answer with "Cat" or "Woof." This better be the answer you are seeking! The effect you were going for will be completely lost if it takes the crowd two minutes to guess the answer you want from them. If you get the right answer, you can use it as a lead-in to the bulk of your speech's intent.

What if?

Paint a picture for your audience and put them in that world.

For example, "Imagine that you jumped out of a plane and discovered that your parachute was broken. What memories flash before your eyes and what regrets are immediate? What if the parachute miraculously opened before you hit the ground and you lived – how would you live your life differently?"

This is similar to the rhetorical question because you paint an alternative reality for them. This is a great way to engage immediately because the "what if" scenario is universal and will make your audience think, regardless of who asks it, period.

If all else fails, just remember two points for your opener.

First, if you're not funny, don't try to use humor. It's something you can practice, but don't practice it in front of a live crowd. It may very well poison your audience's receptivity to the rest of your talk. Use humor very carefully if you aren't good at it.

Second, think about the way your favorite movies begin. They likely start in the middle of a tense or exciting situation like a car chase or hostage negotiation. You may not immediately know what's going on, but the action engages you and encourages you to pay attention to solve the mystery.

Movie openings make you pause and pay attention so you can make sense of it all. Or it's such a big explosion that you can't help taking

notice because it takes up the entire screen.
Neither of those are bad descriptors for your
opener.

Chapter 3. Knowing Your Audience is Key

Kevin Hart is one of my favorite comedians.

Everyone at the top of their respective field has been exceedingly intentional and deliberate about their rise to the top. But Kevin Hart is on a different level.

Allow me to explain.

Kevin Hart understands the value of knowing his audience, so much so that he goes through a particularly tedious vetting process to decide which jokes he delivers on his various national tours.

In other words, different jokes play better in different places. Jokes that might get a huge laugh in some areas of the country (or world) will fall flat in other areas of the country (or world). When you think about it, it's actually a very intuitive thing to do. After all, you wouldn't make jokes about the French if you were in France, would you? And you wouldn't find the same roster of jokes told on BET (Black Entertainment Television) as you would on Oxygen (television programming specifically aimed toward women).

Kevin Hart has assembled a roster of jokes that play well anywhere he goes – they are universal and relatable enough that every group or population finds them humorous.

When you know your audience, you can tailor your presentation or speech in a way that matters to them specifically and will reach them. Like Kevin Hart, you can find the funniest jokes for each audience, or you can find the most staggering statistics or anecdotes for each audience. It's the exact same process.

For many people, their presentation content doesn't change because their underlying assumption is that their audience will always be the same – the only thing that might change is the venue and the scheduling. It's a mindset borne out of laziness and inexperience.

Even the band that plays live shows every night knows their performance has to change based on their audience. There is always interplay between the performer and the audience.

More old-timers are going to tonight's show? We'd better bring back our classics and not stack fast songs right next to each other. More young adults are coming tomorrow? We'd better make sure we're playing our upbeat songs frequently and loudly.

All of this applies handily to your next performance or speech.

Make it your job to your know audience!

Obviously, the more due diligence you perform, the better you will be prepared. Find out what kind of person is in the audience so you can better tailor your message for them. If you don't bother with this part of your preparation, you're actually doing your audience a big disservice and not giving them the respect they deserve.

Advanced spreadsheets and analyses aren't necessary, and you don't need a private investigator. You can just ask the event organizer about the type of person that will be attending and then make educated guesses regarding their preferences.

What information can you ask for?

- Education level
- Age range
- Geographical background
- Industries
- Careers
- Where they read their news (this uncovers political leanings and familiarity with different perspectives)
- Hobbies
- General interests
- What drew people to this event
- What current events they might care about
- Who else they may have heard recently

These are very important pieces of information because they can tell you how to skew or position your presentation. If you can't get hard data points, gather as much circumstantial or inferential evidence as possible about your audience.

Once you have this information, what do you change? Take Kevin Hart's cue.

You change the jokes you tell – more conservative, raunchy, lowbrow, or highbrow. You tell different stories – if you have a more affluent audience, you can tell stories about your gardener or pool, but if you have a poorer audience, you can tell stories about going hungry and not having new shoes.

You change the way you speak – you use a bigger vocabulary at a university alumni event than you might at a seminar on earning your GED. You modulate your vocal intonation, body language, and energy level.

You even change your value proposition and main message if it's applicable. For example, if you're speaking on a general topic of financial security, your message will be geared toward investments and savings for older people, but bank accounts and salary negotiation for younger people.

Maintain an air of respect for your audience by knowing them and what is currently motivating them. If you can't adequately explain your message, the fault lies on you for not tailoring your message with enough clarity.

The biggest benefit to knowing your audience is actually none of the above. When you know your audience, you can demonstrate to them that you

understand who they are and how they think –
and how do you think that comes across to them?

Imagine two people speaking about success and
pulling themselves up from their bootstraps. The
first person was raised in the inner city, had a
single parent household, and studied every day
during their two-hour bus commute to a
renowned high school. The second person had
parents who were both doctors, and received a
corvette for their 16th birthday.

Who do you think has more credibility and is more
likely to be listened to? The one that is relatable
and understands the audience they are speaking
to. You can always *tell* people that you can relate
to them, you can always tell people that you feel
their pain, but that is not going to move the
needle all that far.

Don't just say it; demonstrate it through every
aspect of how you present yourself. Offer stories
or anecdotes that highlight the fact that you
understand what they are thinking and what their
lives are really like.

The greater perception of similarity you can
create, the more people will see you as "one of
their own" and begin to hang on your every word.
Even if your words or ideas are foreign, they'll be

more willing to listen because of your personal familiarity.

Finally, knowing your audience can save you from catastrophe, for example, making an innocent joke about your deceased mother in a cancer support group.

Knowing your audience is another piece of preparation that you should prioritize almost as highly as your presentation itself. Act accordingly.

Chapter 4. Find Your Core Message and Catchphrase

For any speaker or presenter, the Holy Grail is to achieve memorability.

You might be pleased with how a presentation or speech has gone, but if no one remembers it the next day, or no one ever puts anything in practice or use, it's as good as forgotten.

David Eagleman once wrote that everyone dies twice – first when we stop breathing, and second when your name is mentioned for the last time. How can you ensure that your speech doesn't die both times and is actually memorable?

For maximum memorability, you need to distill and condense your core message into a catchphrase. By creating a catchphrase, people will not only be able to remember it more quickly, they'll be able to understand your ideas more easily.

First of all, what's a catchphrase? Well, here are some of the more recognizable ones in western culture:

"Ayyyy!" – The Fonz, from *Happy Days* (a television show that ran from 1974-1984).

"Hasta la vista, baby." – *Terminator 2: Judgment Day* (1991 motion picture).

"Whatchoo talkin' 'bout, Willis?" — *Diff'rent Strokes* (a television show that ran from 1978-1986)

"D'oh!" — *The Simpsons* (a television show that appears to be immortal, running from 1989-present)

And finally,

"I'm Rick James, bitch!" – *Chappelle's Show* (a television show that ran from 2003-2006)

But these aren't catchphrases you can readily incorporate in a presentation or speech. The types of catchphrases you should be focusing on and trying to create are more similar to what Tim Ferriss and Ramit Sethi have created. Their respective catchphrases are "The Four Hour Work Week" and "I Will Teach You to Be Rich." Very succinct, direct, to the point, and informative.

Just as in the previous chapter where Kevin Hart was able to find jokes that would resonate with any audience, this is the process you must do when considering your catchphrase. What kind of approach to your message will actually resonate with any audience, and how can you tailor it?

What Is Your Core Message?

You might have an idea about what your core message and value proposition is, but if you haven't thought about how it relates to your audience, you need to change it. People are attuned to pay attention to things that involve and benefit them, regardless of the topic.

What's in it for them? Let's take Tim Ferriss and Ramit Sethi's catchphrases as examples again. It's very clear why someone would want to listen to them if they have any interest in (1) making money or (2) working less. These are universal themes that nevertheless tie in deeply to their work and content.

So the first step in defining your core message is to think about the value of your message to people's self-interest. It doesn't need to be as concrete as making money or working less, but there has to be a reason people should want to hear it.

Is your main value proposition to give information, to inform, to give advice, to entertain, to make people feel positive emotion, or something else? It's up to you to decide on a macro level what value you bring to people.

Now comes the even harder part. Reduce it to one sentence.

This is going to take some time, but if you aren't able to do this in some fashion, it means your message is jumbled and confusing for listeners.

Think of the process as a Japanese haiku poem – a form that only uses seventeen syllables, yet can say so much. Streamline your core message and the way it appeals to people.

Once you can do that, take it to the next step. Break down that one sentence into five or fewer words. This is crucial because it is not just five random words. They are five words that are related to the catchphrase related to the overall effect you want the audience to have of your speech. Keep working into breaking it down into fewer and fewer words, but keep in mind the overall effect you want those words to bring to the table.

Your goal is to break down your core message in such a way that when people refer to your talk or to you, they will think of you as that catchphrase guy. You want them to identify you with your catchphrase. This makes your core message memorable and easier to process. This leads to your message being more effective overall.

Now that you have gone through the heavy lifting of boiling down your message to answer the classic question *"Why should I care?"* the next step is to drill it into the minds of your audience members.

The easiest way to do this is simply to repeat your catchphrase throughout your presentation. If you've ever watched the comedian Chris Rock, you've noticed that he does this quite a bit. He repeats himself constantly throughout his set so he can set the stage for what he is going to talk about. He tells you the catchphrase, then explains it a bit. He tells you again, explains it more, and carries on in this manner until the end of the joke when he again tells you the catchphrase to wrap it all together.

As a result, Chris Rock has some of the most repeatable lines and jokes in all of comic history – unfortunately, they aren't phrases I can repeat in this book.

He is a genius for recognizing that people have very short attention spans and respond best to repetition. If you thought only children and animals respond to that, then you far overestimated how different we are from them.

Repetition also has the benefit of allowing you to talk about more complex concepts. Repeating your main points reminds the audience of where you are and where you came from, and allows you to go deeper.

After hashing out your core message, make sure there are three main takeaways from it. No more, no less. Most people make the mistake of erring on more, but that just jumbles your message and causes people to forget. If you ask someone to remember a phone number, they might only remember three or four of the digits. But if you ask someone to remember only the three-digit area code, there's no chance they'll forget it.

Focus on three and leave it. Again, if you can't articulate your core message and tenets in three points and have to keep using *ifs, ands, and buts*, your message is jumbled.

Remember how Steve Jobs introduced the original iPhone? In three simple components – a phone, the Internet, and the iPod (mobile music player).

Anytime you're speaking, the goal is to have others talk about your speech. To make it easier for them, make yourself sound bites. This is similar to your core message, but a sound bite is just a phrase, sentence, or concept that is easily shareable. In a sense, it can go viral, and is very quotable.

For example, when I speak to people and clients, I always use phrases that I believe are highly quotable, which makes them stick in people's minds. A couple of mine are "Know your stories," and "Filler words feel like chemistry."

The more compact and hard-hitting a catchphrase is, the higher the likelihood that your audience members will share that quote and keep you memorable.

A final method to drive your core message and

catchphrase home is to give the audience a call to action. In other words, give them something they can do immediately (or in the very near future) that is related to your core message and catchphrase.

Your presentation might be touching on themes of impossibility and perseverance. You can ask your audience to attempt to lick their own nose, or lick their own elbow. Something about tying a core message together with a physical act makes it exponentially more memorable and more likely to resonate.

Catchphrases can be difficult to create, but the real challenge lies in making them stick in people's minds.

Chapter 5. Standup Comics are Performance Gurus

Standup comics might not be the first people that come to mind when you think of a public speaking master... but they should be.

Standup comics are performance gurus in ways that we can only dream about – the biggest reason is because every time they step on stage, it's a battle.

It's a battle because they are going out on stage to get laughs, evoke emotions, and ultimately win the crowd over. It's also one of the most difficult things in the world to do – captivate a crowd and make them laugh on command for an hour straight.

When you or I step onto stage, our goals are never that large. Most of the time we just want people to smile, take a note or two, and remember that we were even a part of their day.

But standup comics are literally trying to hit a home run every single time. They don't just want to evoke emotion – they want to evoke huge, subjective emotions that can make people's stomachs and cheeks hurt from laughing. The upside they are swinging for is huge, and their potential downside is also amazingly huge.

They willingly open themselves up to extreme judgment from their audience, and comedy is a setting in which heckling, jeering, and booing are commonplace and accepted. The worst we'll get is a lukewarm applause and exasperated sighs.

And despite it all, standup comics have the commitment to go out and do it for nights in a row to perfect their jokes.

So what can we learn from standup comics besides a freakish rejection of rejection itself and perseverance?

Entertainment

First, their primary objective is to entertain. If you can entertain an audience, you will have them in the palm of your hand, and they will be captive to anything you say. How many times have you let someone have their way, or even do whatever they want, just because they're entertaining?

Even if you are talking about a more serious subject matter, your audience will respond better if you are entertaining. If you have a lesson, they'll absorb if better if they are having a good time listening to you. If you are presenting statistics, they'll understand them better if you can analogize your findings to Beatles albums. No matter your purpose, it will work better if you make your primary focus entertaining for the audience.

It's like interpersonal and social skills – if you tweak your goal to create an entertaining interaction, things like job offers and connections follow naturally. Create an entertaining experience on the stage and your secondary goals will follow naturally.

Delivery

Second point: the delivery of a standup comic is breathtaking when you break it down.

They've mastered comedic timing. They've mastered how to react to a crowd and get reactions from them. They've mastered what facial expressions and simple grunts will get laughs over others. They wait for the crowd to pay attention.

Every pause, stutter, and show of frustration is intentional. They may seem spontaneous and random (concepts I will cover later), but these professionals have rehearsed these situations to squeeze the utmost emotional reaction from them.

Memorization

Standup comics are 100% off book, which means that they never look at their notes. They realize how big a barrier notes can be between them and the audience, and how it breaks any bond they might develop with them.

This may seem daunting at first, but it's a matter of practice and memorization through memory palaces, which is a concept I cover later. It is easier than you think. By focusing first on memorizing general points and concepts, you can then start fleshing out the rest of your talk based on the items you memorized.

It also allows them to take over the stage and move from end to end, which makes them instantly more interesting to the audience than if they were just standing still.

Audience Specificity

Even though I think Kevin Hart is a top comic and his revenue would agree, he's not an international success. In fact, there are very few comics that ever become internationally successful, and there is a good reason for this.

When you watch an action movie, you don't really need to speak the local language and know the culture. A gunshot is a gunshot and an explosion is an explosion in any part of the world. These transcend language and cultural barriers. Comedy, on the other hand, is too culturally specific.

There are still many hoops a comedian has to go through to make his material apply across borders as far as cultural differences go. This illustrates the fact that if you want to be an effective speaker, you have to make sure your speech is context and audience specific. Know your audience. Fine-tune your material to speak directly to the needs of your audience as well as the overall context of why they showed up to listen to your speech.

Self-deprecation

The root of why many people are drawn to presenting and public speaking is ego. There's no shame in that. You do it because it makes you feel prestigious and influential.

But to be an effective speaker, you need to be discrete.

Arrogance and ego are two things that audiences hate and have no problem mercilessly booing. If an audience senses that you take yourself too seriously, are condescending, or have an unfounded high opinion of yourself, they'll let you know how they feel about it.

On the other hand, standup comics are the first to laugh at themselves. In fact, they often make long jokes about their own negative qualities. Besides being funny and entertaining, it lets the audience know that they don't take themselves too seriously, and can laugh at themselves.

It disarms an audience and lets them know it's okay to laugh and be themselves without holding back, and when you think about it, the opposite is very, very uncomfortable.

Fearless Transitions

Comedians transition from joke to joke quickly and fearlessly. Often, this is out of necessity because jokes are usually on completely different topics, as opposed to a keynote speech focused solely on, say, perseverance or any other topic.

But the point here is that transitions should be quick and fearless. They aren't aspects of your presentation on which you need to spend undue amounts of time.

There are two main ways comics transition between topics. First, they will do it in one sentence and simply say, "So, have you guys heard about X?" Fearless and without shame, and it gets the job done. Continuity matters less than you might think.

The second way is to finish a topic, launch into what appears to be a related personal anecdote, but the anecdote actually leads to the next topic. For example, "Phones... my son is attached to his phone, and he's five years old. He texts me when I'm in the next room to ask me to change the channel for him. Phone addiction is becoming a big problem in society, and studies have shown..."

Word Economy

Comics don't waste a single word because they know too many or too few can spell death for a joke's punch line.

The best comics tend to keep things short, compact, and punchy. This is by design. If your jokes have many parts to them or they tend to be very long, the likelihood that people might not get the key points of your joke increases. If you don't express your idea with clarity within a certain number of words, the expression is lost.

Learn how to make your point immediately or tease it out with your delivery. Regardless, the fewer words you force yourself to use, the higher the likelihood your message will be clear.

The Callback

A callback is when a comic integrates a joke he made earlier into his current joke. For example, if the comic made a joke earlier about dogs, and his current joke is about rollercoasters, a callback would be a humorous way to refer to the dogs in the context of rollercoasters.

First joke: dogs are actually secret agents posing as unintelligent.

Current joke: rollercoasters are a way for

amusement parks to make money from things falling out of people's pockets.

Callback: would a dog fasten itself into a seatbelt or sacrifice itself to maintain its air of stupidity?

It's usually hilarious because combining elements of two jokes is powerful, and it shows an attention to detail that you might call clever wit.

Learn how to effectively use a callback in your own presentation, whether it's with a joke, referencing a story, something an audience member said, or just the opener you used in the beginning to break the ice.

Chapter 6. How to Make an Emotional Impact

Think back to the last movie that made you laugh, cry, or feel furious at injustice.

You may not remember exactly the circumstances that made you feel that way, but I'll bet you remember feeling that way, and sometimes that is more important than remembering the specifics.

The same easily applies to your presentations or speeches. If you can make someone feel emotionally connected to you and spike their emotions, you will be instantly memorable. You may not care that people remember the nuances of your points or how articulate your closing was – when we present, we just want to make an impact and have people remember us. Emotions are how people feel connected to you as a speaker and as a person.

Even if you are giving a talk that is completely objective and involves very dry subject matter, you still need to make an emotional impact. People have an easier time understanding a particular concept if they are able to relate to it on an emotional level. Regardless of how important the information is, all will be lost in translation if people simply couldn't relate.

For example, you can speak dryly about the retirement age skyrocketing in most western countries, and the lack of social services to account for them. It's a terrible situation, but you can make the proper emotional impact by asking people about their own grandparents and the struggles they'll have in the coming years.

We'd like to believe that we're logical and driven by data and science, but deep down we make many decisions by emotion alone (and then come up with a rationalized explanation for our decision after the fact – but that's a phenomenon for another book).

Your talk has to make an emotional impact for you to become a great speaker, presenter, or performer. Otherwise, it's just not going to be all that effective. Always come back to the fact that people may not always remember what you say or do, but they will definitely remember how you made them feel.

There are many different ways to create an emotional impact. The only limit, really, is your imagination because, as mentioned before, there are many different types of audiences out there. They bring different experiences and emotional triggers to the table and there are many different contexts, so they have many different ways of connecting to a piece of information.

Tell Stories

There's a reason movies hit home emotionally so often. They are stories designed to draw you into one person's perspective and make you walk a mile in their shoes. They can use this access and power for negative or positive emotions; standup comics use the same power of telling stories about ridiculous situations to evoke laughter.

When you're telling a story, make sure to talk about relatable situations and emotions so your audience can easily identify with you and jump into your shoes. Use common situations, obstacles, and insecurities to really hammer home your point.

For example, if you wanted to talk about why wages should be raised, you can use a cold approach like speaking about the rising income gap between the poor and the rich. That's an argument that is statistically heavy and not very compelling. People may be surprised at the statistics, but there won't be any emotional impact.

For a better way to speak about why wages should be raised, you could weave a story about an individual named Craig who is struggling on the low wages he earns. You would talk about how every month he has to choose which bills to pay, how he subsists on mostly beans and rice, and how his children get made fun of at school for not wearing decent clothes.

Which has the greater impact and will drive someone to action? You tell me.

Any time you can talk about the human condition and how it relates to your point, you need to use it to your advantage.

Colorful, personal, and specific metaphors drive home the same point. They're just an abbreviated story that will allow people to relate to your point quickly and personally.

Project Passion and Conviction

You can create emotional impact simply by looking and acting emotional. Speak with passion and conviction. Don't hide how you feel about certain topics. Ask yourself what you are trying to convey and make sure to convey it with your words and expressions.

Emotions are very infectious and as long as you look authentic and genuine, people can't help feeling affected by you. How many people begin to tear and cry if they even just look at someone who is crying? How many people will begin to smile or laugh if they see someone who is laughing so hard they can't squeeze the words out of their mouth?

Displaying emotion will make people sit up and pay attention because people normally don't get all emotionally worked up about something unless it's important. They'll try to understand you based on their emotional vocabulary, which will scream at them.

You can't fake it because if people in the audience detect that you're yanking their chain, it becomes much easier for them to write you off. They'll feel as if you're just putting on an act and this gives them an excuse to discount whatever it is you're saying, so don't overplay passion and conviction. Only use it if you're authentically and genuinely emotionally worked up about what you're talking about.

The Personal Anecdote

The big difference between standard storytelling and a personal anecdote is that with a personal anecdote, the focus is on you only.

You're inviting the audience to step into your world and feel about a certain topic the exact same way you felt, or are still feeling, about it. It's harder for them to sidestep the emotional impact of what you're saying because you're not talking about a theory or a random person who can't live on minimum wage. You're talking about something that exists in a concrete way in front of their faces.

When you open up and make yourself vulnerable to the audience, there is an additional element of bravery and courage that people will impart to you.

Hyperbole and Extremes

There are certain common speech techniques you

can use to increase emotional impact: example, hyperbole, contrast, extremes, allusions, and references.

All these help magnify the subject matter and associated emotions involved. By using these techniques you can give anything an emotional impact, but you have to be careful not to go overboard and become unbelievable and not relatable.

For example, you could compare your boss to Hitler – that would certainly make an emotional impact, but would you be going overboard and lose credibility?

What if you described a new ballot measure as "Literally the worst thing to happen to democracy since communism."? Certainly makes an audience sit up and pay attention.

Finally, what if you talked about effective leadership as "The difference between a billion dollar company and the founders waiting in line for unemployment and social services."?

These are all things that will make an audience innately care about what you have to say.

When you use examples or employ the power of

hyperbole, contrast, extremes, allusions, or use references, you localize the subject matter and give your audience the opportunity to connect emotionally to what you are saying. Tap into their base emotions of happiness, disgust, sadness, fear, and surprise. Imagine your goal is to make someone's face cringe because they can feel that emotion themselves.

In the same vein, you can use extremely vivid and sensory words to take people places mentally. Let your vocabulary do your work for you. For example, instead of saying "great job," what are some more effective phrases you can use?

Pack your phrases full of sensory information to allow people to visualize places and emotions. For example, how might you describe a transition from one job to another? You could say "rough, tough, or a work in progress"... or you could say "like swallowing nails, going as fast as a penguin waddles, or smooth as sandpaper."

Move Closer if Possible

When you lean in as you talk or when you walk closer to your audience, you give a visual signal to audience members that you are somebody to be trusted. There is a correlation between the amount of space separating the speaker and the audience, and the emotional reception of the speaker by the audience.

According to Edward T. Hall's classic work, *The Silent Language*, there are four zones of personal space between people. Use them to your advantage in creating the impression of intimacy.

If you are speaking to a crowd of people and there are twelve or more feet separating you from them, people in the audience will perceive that space as public space. There's not much emotional electricity there.

When you reduce that space from twelve to four feet, the audience members will feel that you're communicating with them at a social level. You are a bit more intimate and it's easier for them to connect with you emotionally at this distance.

When you reduce the space from four feet to a foot and a half, they will feel you are in their personal space. It's much easier to make an emotional connection here, but if you say the wrong thing, or if you act the wrong way, it's also very easy to be perceived as threatening or intimidating.

Finally, according to Hall, if you are standing a foot and a half to zero feet in front of the audience, you are well into their intimate space. In many cases, this is completely inappropriate unless they are so emotionally worked up already because you've gradually stepped into more and more intimate space and can get away throwing catchphrases that really punctuate the emotional highpoints of your talk.

It's important to be aware of these four zones of personal space so you can use them for maximum emotional impact.

Humor?

When you use an element of humor and comic relief it makes people feel more comfortable and enjoy you more.

But as I've mentioned, if you aren't funny, don't try to be funny. If you attempt it, here are a few ways to make sure your attempts at humor convey what you want.

First, select your jokes very carefully. It has to be clear to the audience that you are joking. If you are ambiguous about the joke, or make vague references, they might think you're serious – or just confusing.

Second, only certain types of humor translate well

on stage. For example, sarcasm might be great when you're talking to your friends or people who have known you for a long time. But not all types of sarcasm will go over well if you tell these types of jokes to a large group of strangers.

Finally, resist the urge to explain your joke. Just move on. You had a crack and it missed, so don't belabor the point. If you made a joke and only a few people laughed, don't double up on your failure by explaining it. Explaining the joke only hammers home your failure and draws out the moment of awkwardness. Rarely has explaining a joke produced more laughs than were there originally.

Chapter 7. Project Your Emotions

When you're performing or presenting in front of people, chances are you will be some distance away (up on a stage, for example). You may also feel that you are not as well amplified as you'd like.

Technical difficulties aside, this means that not everything you do during a normal conversation will work when you're on stage. Specifically, the non-verbal ways you usually rely on to show emotion or your reactions to things needs to be calibrated differently when you're on stage.

When you're speaking to someone who is five feet away in a normal conversation, you might wrinkle your mouth or raise an eyebrow to demonstrate skepticism – but that won't work onstage because you're too far removed from your audience.

If you're used to making small side comments or relying on subtle facial expressions to convey your emotions, you're also out of luck. These won't fly on stage!

Imagine how small you are in the context of a big stage, in front of a big curtain, in a huge auditorium or theater. Clearly your emotions must grow commensurately with the setting and become exaggerated if you want to successfully convey your ideas.

Although it may be enough to frown just a little bit when you are with a friend for your friend to get that you are sad, on stage you need to go over the top. You have to make an extra effort to visibly display your emotions.

What's ironic about this is that internally you might feel you are hamming it up in front of your audience, but when they look at you they feel you're not projecting enough emotion. You have to look at your emotions through the eyes of your audience. Consider how they perceive your emotional range. Simply assuming that your normal emotional display is sufficient is not going to cut it.

Energy Level

The first step to making sure you are conveying your emotions successfully is to keep your energy level higher than you normally would. A good rule of thumb is to keep it at least one to two notches above that of the audience's.

It's just the nature of the beast. If you come on stage with a low energy level and don't show any enthusiasm, you'll lose your audience before you say a word.

But my point is more about being aware that you must elevate your energy level. If you think you're at a 10, your audience will perceive a 5.

If you want them to see you at a 10, you'll have to push yourself to a 15 even though that will seem overly dramatic to you.

If you are feeling emotional about your talk, it's important to kick it up or your audience won't feel the same way you do. They won't feel the emotional urgency you're trying to convey.

Use Your Voice with Force

The same goes for your voice and the vocal inflection you use on stage.

You must inject life and energy into your voice because your voice is the primary way people will get clues regarding the emotions they should be feeling about what you're talking about. What you do in normal conversation won't work, so this is another case of kicking it up a notch to successfully convey your emotion or intent.

Use a lot of vocal inflection paired with a lot of gestures. This may feel to you as if you're overreacting, or overacting, but you're really not. Rule of thumb: the bigger the emotion you want to communicate, the bigger your gestures should be.

Coordinate your facial expressions and body language with your emotions. Imagine you can't speak and the only way you have to convey a message to someone is with your facial expressions. Your cheeks, eyebrows, and eyes would probably be sore afterwards because you'd strain them communicating your message.

This way, the emotion you're projecting is unmistakable and unambiguous.

Control Your Tics

People tend to fall back on a variety of crutches when they are feeling stressed.

If you are giving a speech and you're intimidated by your crowd, it's likely you'll start saying "Um," "Like," or "You know," more than you should in an effort to collect your thoughts and buy time while you figure out what you want to say. You're editing your speech in real time.

Physically, you might twitch, fidget, shift your weight from side to side, or literally shake.

These are all nervous tics and are dead giveaways to your audience that you are nervous and uncomfortable.

They also take away from the emotion you want to project and make the audience uncomfortable for you. Here's a secret: the audience wants you to succeed for a variety of reasons, but mostly because if you don't, they feel incredibly uncomfortable. This is the familiar face-palming cringe that we all sometimes feel. So if you don't get these tics under control, discomfort will overshadow any emotion you want to convey.

Speak Slowly

Adrenaline, cortisol, and other hormones that stress cause make your heart race. This means that without intending to, you will probably speak much faster on stage than you normally would. It's a proven phenomenon that if you think you are speaking at a rate of X, you are probably speaking at a rate of 1.5X on stage.

To combat this, try to speak at .5X on stage so that you end up speaking at a rate that resembles normal speech.

By consciously slowing down your speech pattern, you will be able to take full control of the emotional message you're sending out.

This is actually one of the main tenets of public speaking and performing, and if you've done any amount of reading on this topic, you're already aware of it, so I won't beat that poor dead horse.

Establish Eye Contact

As you are speaking slowly to your audience and trying to paint an emotional picture, or draw them into your emotional state, establish eye contact.

Depending on your context and setup, it may be difficult to see your audience because of the lights pointed directly at you.

If at all possible, pick a specific person to make eye contact with. Depending on the size of your venue, you can probably divide the audience into at least six distinct areas (three in front, three in back). Pick a specific spot or person within each of those areas to make eye contact with for a minute or two. Then move on. Make sure everyone feels engaged and connected and involved.

Even though you have rehearsed and planned this, you will still look spontaneous and engaged with your audience. Imagine trying to connect emotionally with an audience with your head buried in your notes, not looking up or at anyone. It's quite a contrast.

Watch Yourself

Yes, it's uncomfortable, and you might hate it. But watching yourself and knowing how you appear from the perspective of the audience is the only way you can truly improve how you project your emotions and your stage presence in general.

I've saved the best for last.

By watching yourself on video, you can see exactly what's in your emotional toolbox. What do you convey well, and what do you convey poorly? Do you fidget constantly to the point of distraction, or do you look too much like a statue? These are just some of the things you should watch for during the postmortem tape of your presentation.

You will gain a very clear idea of how to improve your emotional messaging when you see yourself in action. An effective litmus test is to turn off the sound and just watch your facial expressions and body language. Can you tell what emotion you are trying to get across? Or are your non-verbal expressions too muted and subdued to decipher?

If you can't make out the emotions or intentions, keep practicing that emotional signal until it's loud and clear. One of the best ways to do this is to practice in front of a mirror. Break down the basic emotions of happiness, sadness, fear, anger, surprise and disgust and try to express them in front of the mirror without saying a word. Rely heavily on your facial expressions, eyes, eyebrows, cheeks, gestures, body language, foot positioning, and anything else at your disposal – everything!

Is the emotion you see in the mirror the same as the emotion you're sending out and, as important, the one you meant to send out?

Practice in front of the mirror until you can convey

certain basic emotions without saying a single word. Now imagine how much more you need to exaggerate them to make them conveyable (or even visible) on stage.

Feel silly? Five hours of silliness in front of the mirror by yourself passes more quickly than ten seconds of awkward silence and chatter from your audience when you're on stage.

Chapter 8. Rehearse Your Spontaneity

Without fail, whenever a head of state such as a president or prime minister addresses the nation, it is incredibly rehearsed.

I don't necessarily mean that in a positive manner, but I can't blame them. The objective for a head of state is to show perfection, and any stutter or flub has the potential to completely destroy their public image. Case in point, George W. Bush, a former President of the United States who was infamous for his word flubs and how they made everyone devalue his intelligence.

The stakes are so high that heads of state effectively remove any semblance of emotion or spontaneity from their delivery.

That's where you should be different in your delivery. We've already covered how to infuse your presentation or performance with more emotion and conviction, but what about spontaneity?

Spontaneity in presentation doesn't literally mean you just wing it and say whatever comes to mind regardless of the consequences. It means that the opposite – appearing overly rehearsed – makes you appear not relatable, stiff, and boring. It's an unattractive quality in a presenter, period.

The best speakers are those who look as if they're speaking from the heart, are passionate, engaged, and moved by a feeling.

Compare the raw power of Martin Luther King, Jr. giving his "I have a dream" speech from the steps of the Lincoln Memorial versus a subdued keynote speech by a president or prime minister. Or in a more normal context, compare someone who is so rehearsed they just go through the motions; their eyes glaze over in a kind of highway hypnosis, and they finish through habit and instinct alone, versus someone who tells you a funny story that just happened to them. Which do you think will be more compelling and engaging?

Spontaneity is a key aspect of engaging presentations and performances. When was the last time you got excited about someone reading from a teleprompter? When you appear spontaneous, you attack each sentence, phrase, and story in a far different manner.

An audience perceives spontaneity extremely well, and while I'm not proposing you go off-script or speak whimsically, you do need to make sure you don't seem robotic and rehearsed. If you are too rehearsed, you send a bad message to your audience. They will think you view your talk as a chore. You won't come off as if you're actually enjoying talking to them.

When you're spontaneous, on the other hand, it loosens up the crowd and it also loosens you up. The more relaxed you appear, the more relaxed the crowd feels. Eventually you create a pleasant flow that feels more like a conversation and a dialogue and not like you're delivering a sermon from a pulpit.

Again, standup comics understand this flow and utilize it to the best of their abilities. They are the very definition of rehearsed spontaneity.

Their entire act is premised on being natural,

telling stories, and having a conversation with the audience. And yet, they aren't actually being spontaneous at all. Make no mistake about it; every stutter, eye roll, groan, pause, or seemingly spontaneous act on their part is extremely well-rehearsed. The bottom line is they know how to *appear* spontaneous, and that makes them funny, engaging, and anything but boring.

If you appear spontaneous, they'll feel your wit, intelligence, and ease with speaking are all natural. You don't have to tell them you rehearsed continually to appear spontaneous. What's important is that you're perceived as spontaneous.

The ability to have rehearsed spontaneity is actually a testament to a whole new level of mastery over your material. If you know your material only adequately, you'll appear rehearsed and stiff because you won't feel secure enough to make it natural and yours. You'll stick to the script because if you don't, you might lose your train of thought entirely. You won't be able to think as well on the next level – how you present yourself and how you are perceived – because you'll have to focus on the material itself.

It's as if you are just basically memorizing key parts so that you can retain information you have only a slippery grasp of. What is the solution? Very simple, master your material. The more you know your material, the more you can experiment with pacing, and the more spontaneous you will look.

When you know your content backwards and forwards, it's very easy for you to look relaxed and appear spontaneous. Having that level of knowledge and confidence in your material will allow you to seem as if you've let your hair down and are playing around with your material. That's the kind of mastery rehearsed spontaneity requires.

The essence of rehearsed spontaneity is simple. You have such a command over the material that you can take comments in stride, explore tangents, and even go completely off script if you wish. You'll be able to stride around the stage and integrate audience questions into the material, and generally appear natural as if you were explaining how to tie a shoelace.

Spontaneity is an impression you're trying to create. It's never true spontaneity because the perception comes from complete, off-notes mastery of your material. The more you know your stuff, the more prepared you are, and the more work you put into rehearsing, the more spontaneous you will appear. Your wit quotient will skyrocket because you'll have a response for anything involving your material because you know it so well.

If there's one analogy that best summarizes the power of rehearsed spontaneity, think of jazz music.

Jazz music is one of the most complex types of music to play because there are so many different scales and modalities – and the vast majority of it is mostly improvisational. On the surface, it is the epitome of rehearsed spontaneity. Your mastery of the scales and modalities is so powerful that although you're not exactly being spontaneous, you have the natural passion of someone who is. Little does your audience know that you've put in hundreds, if not thousands, of hours mastering those scales so that everything they hear looks natural and every note fits just right.

Chapter 9. The Power of Stage Presence

Stage presence is a term that's hard to quantify, which is why the usual terms to describe it are literally "the *it* factor," "the X factor," or simply a certain *je ne sais quoi*. Instead of describing what stage presence is, it makes more sense to describe how it makes an audience feel.

A performer or presenter with stage presence has the type of charisma that draws the audience in and demands their full attention. It doesn't come from being overbearingly loud or aggressive – it's a quality that makes people not want to miss a second of you on stage.

You become magnetic to people's eyes and draw

them in; it's what separates the good, fundamentally sound speakers from the transcendent ones. You become, in a sense, larger than life. People will watch, captivated, as if in a trance.

In my opinion, the performer with the most stage presence was the late Freddie Mercury, lead singer of the band Queen. I implore you to investigate his live performances in the 1980s. It is extremely apparent that he has the audience eating out of the palm of his hand. It's a spectacle to watch Freddie waltz nonchalantly across the stage in a skintight white leotard, dance with his microphone, and dance wildly. Sometimes he's in his own world, and sometimes he speaks directly to the audience and plays with them.

You can't take your eyes off of him.

The good news is, you can break down many components of what he did, and what other magnetic stage performers do. It will take practice to cultivate, but it will help you if you don't own a white leotard.

Here are a few things Freddie and other high performers do to maximize their stage presence.

Cover the Stage

The first step to maximizing your stage presence is to take full ownership of the stage.

The moment you get up there, make it yours. People take notice of this.

Don't just stay at your podium and turn your head occasionally to the audience.

In the hoped for circumstance that you are not anchored to the podium, but have a portable microphone, walk the stage and own that space. Always make sure to face the crowd and never turn your back to them. Talk to different sections of the audience at different points, and vary your walking speed to emphasize your point. Engage from all angles.

When you're pivoting around the whole stage, people can't help but pay attention to you – you're unavoidable. You make it personal for each sector you're close to, and if the spotlight isn't too bright, you'll literally be able to see the "head nodding" effect you're having on the people closest to the stage.

From a visual standpoint, it also helps prevent boredom. If you're just standing in one fixed spot, it's easy for people to become visually bored. But if you're moving around, their eyes are engaged and you are demanding to be heard. Just don't pace around manically as if you don't have the ability to stand still.

Interact Personally

Address your audience. If you know the names of anyone in the audience, use them. Look people in the eye and speak to them as a whole.

Involve your audience. Freddie Mercury played the echo game with his audiences – he would sing a phrase, then encourage the audience to sing it back to him. After a few rounds, he was able to use the audience as backup singers for any number of Queen's hits. How can you involve your audience in a similar way? Ask for ideas or assertions. Ask them to complete your sentences. Tell a humorous story and ask if anyone has anything similar.

On the other end of the spectrum, Tony Robbins, renowned life and business coach, engages his audience with non-verbal participation. He regularly has physical and breathing exercises during his workshops, and dance segments aren't a rarity for how well they energize and personally involve an audience.

Maintain High Energy Throughout

Despite what I said about there being multiple ways to create a captivating stage presence, the one common thread is that you can't have a low energy level.

It doesn't mean there are no long silences or intentional pauses in your speech, but people must be able to see that there's a lot of energy even in those pauses. Performing shouldn't be all that relaxing physically – you should be sweating when you walk off the stage.

If you're awakened from sleep by someone, are you more likely to fully wake up if that person as just as sleepy, or if they are already fully awake themselves? On the other hand, you are likely to find someone who is disproportionately and (almost) inappropriately energetic off-putting and annoying, so there is a fine line you have to find in terms of your stage energy level.

You can't overdo it because when you go over that line, you go from being a person that's credible, and worth listening to, to an attention-seeker.

Amplify and exaggerate emotions, but don't come off as an obnoxious attention seeker. Otherwise, whatever you do is going to be perceived as fake.

Just keep this simple rubric in mind: what kind of puppy are you most likely to get excited about?

Create a Stage Persona

Creating a stage persona is exactly what it sounds like.

This is a costume and mask that you don for the stage that does all the things you aren't completely confident or comfortable in doing. This persona is amazingly outrageous, nonchalant, and powerful.

Once you step into that character, you can do things that the normal you could never do! It's empowering, and is similar to why studies have found an increase in crime on Halloween. People feel incredible freedom at the prospect of wearing a costume and mask; it allows them to drop their inhibitions and act on their desires.

You can channel this in a positive way. The starker the contrast between your persona and your real personality the better. If you are calm, collected, and cool, then your stage persona should be larger than life and outrageous. Name your stage persona – even Beyoncé did it when she created her stage persona, Sasha Fierce.

What's something you've always wanted to do on stage? Maybe Patrick wouldn't do that, but Patrick's stage persona Kingston Jupiter III has no problem with it! Once you see that it can be okay for someone else to do something else on stage, it slowly makes it more acceptable for you to do it in your normal persona.

If you step into someone else's shoes, you can shed the shackles of self-consciousness and embody everything that even Freddie Mercury was.

Watch and Learn

Watch your favorite music acts and performers! Simply pay attention to when you are engrossed in what's happening on stage, and what the lead singer or guitarist is doing to create that effect.

Watch and learn. Take notes about their performance and try to imagine yourself doing it. If you can't, try to imagine yourself doing it to a lesser degree. Eventually, you'll find the intersection where your personal style can integrate the stage presence of famous acts.

Create Comfort

You might not believe it, but every single audience wants you to do well. If you don't, you make them uncomfortable and tense. People may enjoy watching car crashes, but not when it comes to personal embarrassment.

So how do you keep your audience comfortable with your stage presence? Come prepared!

Chapter 10. Always Be Storytelling

I studied psychology in college, and in that curriculum there were a few classes on neurobiology.

I had a particularly engaging professor who loved to tell stories to illustrate points, and it was quite effective in promoting memorization.

You have both rods and cones in your eyes. Rods are the light receptors that distinguish shades of grey (including black), and cones are the light receptors that distinguish colors. This might seem like an odd bit of information for me to have right at the top of my head, but I've remembered it for over a decade because of the story my professor told us about rods and cones.

He told a complicated story about how his knowing the difference between rods and cones saved his life one dark, stormy night when he was in a car accident.

In hindsight, it probably wasn't a true story, but the point is that storytelling drives home a point more powerfully than anything else. That's why in your presentation or speech, you must always be storytelling.

Storytelling is an extremely effective tool that draws people in and holds their attention for long periods of time.

If you need your own proof of this, think back to the classic sitcom *Seinfeld*. The show, as its creators openly admit, was a show about *nothing*. It was a series of everyday stories that happened to everyday people and occasionally led to a lesson or moral, but Seinfeld was one of the highest grossing and most popular shows in television history. Stories matter.

By focusing on telling great stories, you can engage effectively because our lives are simply made up of these little stories. People put themselves in your shoes and relate through their own lives and experiences.

Storytelling is the best way to plant an idea in someone's mind. It's how people make sense of abstract concepts and really take them to heart. You can blast all sorts of statistics or facts to your audience, but your presentation will start to resemble a school lecture and people will quickly lose interest. If you're able to package these statistics or facts into an illustrative story, it's guaranteed to make a bigger impact and stay in people's memories longer.

There's a reason that Aesop's fables are still known around the world, despite being thousands of years old. Lessons contained in stories stay relevant because of the stories themselves.

If you've ever studied any type of sales or marketing, you've learned the same lesson. When you want to make an impact and really want someone to buy something, using a story that people can relate to will provide the best bang for your buck. For example, imagine hearing a story about someone in your position facing the exact same challenges you face as opposed to a dry listing of your probability of success. There's no question which works better. In short, facts tell, stories sell.

One of the secrets of effective storytelling is detail. The more detail the better.

The more details you use in a story, the more chances there are for people to connect emotionally and be able to relate to the picture you are painting for them. They won't have to expend any effort using their imaginations to be on the same page as you, which makes it easier for you to connect with them in general.

For example, there are two ways to tell a story about your dog. You can mention you had a dog when you were a child, but that he died of cancer. Or, you can mention that you had a golden retriever when you were a child who loved stealing treats out of your pants pockets, who unfortunately died in your arms of cancer.

Which story will people be more likely to connect with? The version with more detail, because if any of those details match their own experience, they will relate instantly. If the detail happens to be something you can match vulnerability on, that's even more powerful. At that point you generate a certain "us versus the world" mentality because of the vulnerable truth you've both experienced.

And besides, it's just plain easier to connect over personal struggles and pains than it is over successes – struggle and pain is more universal and we identify with it more readily.

What are some other uses for storytelling? Almost anything. Stories are never neutral and can always be used to prove a point and push an agenda if you want.

Your stories can show positive traits about you (Did I tell you about the time I saved a baby lamb from death?), emphasize a point in your message (Did I tell the story of how Willy the whale was sadly killed for his blubber?), or make you even more persuasive by showing people things you've done before (Did I tell you about the way I increased revenue by 200% last year?).

Stories are the epitome of "show, don't tell." Anyone can tell you they graduated from a top university or that they won awards, but so what? Telling a story that highlights your expertise and how you are able to connect with clients illustrates your value and immediately elevates you above others with the same boring credentials.

The bottom line with stories is that anyone can use a story to emphasize their point.

For example, take the story of Henry Ford, the inventor of the Model T automobile. He started a car company that failed when it competed with Thomas Edison's company. Then he started a car company that he was booted from. Finally, he started a company that became the Ford Motor Company and successfully revolutionized transportation throughout the world. On top of that, he popularized the assembly line approach to manufacturing, was one of the first proponents of the 40-hour workweek, and was renowned for how well he paid his workers.

If you ever want to talk about themes of persistence, innovation, consistency, overcoming hardships, perseverance, or entrepreneurship, Henry Ford's life is the story for you. You can use it to illustrate to people that failures in business are just as important as successes. The list is endless – how else might you be able to use the story of Henry Ford's life?

You can tweak any kind of story and cherry-pick the details to fit the message you're trying to get across. You should use as many stories as possible because they're great at framing otherwise boring facts, details, and theories into something people can easily relate to on an emotional level.

Finally, remember that there are basic elements of a successful story that you need to have. All stories must have (1) context and description, (2) an action that disrupts the context, and (3) the results of the action on the context.

If any of these elements are missing, your story will probably be anti-climactic, miss the punch line, confusing, or just plain bad.

Context is the framing of the story. Who are the characters? What's the story about? What is the setting? What circumstances will be affected by the ensuing action? (I was skiing with a friend down a black diamond slope. There were lots of trees and forks but luckily we were able to stay pretty close together.)

Action is what takes place in the story. If you're telling a story where there is no action, you don't have much of a story. (Soon we encountered a fork in the slope and we each took a different direction by accident. We lost each other!)

The result is the conclusion of the story and what happened because of the action. (The forks led in entirely different directions and I ended up at the bottom of the hill 20 minutes earlier than my friend did. I couldn't believe it!)

Of course, when you're telling a story and constructing your three elements, make sure you always answer that nagging question that people listening to you ask themselves: "Why should I care?"

Chapter 11. Ethos and Logos

The Greek philosopher Aristotle said that when it comes to persuasion, you can either use ethos, logos, or pathos. Respectively, these Latin terms refer to ethics, logic, and emotion. They are the most powerful ways to make an impact on someone because they are the three most basic aspects that people want to feel fulfilled in.

We've already covered the value of appealing to emotion (pathos) to make a compelling argument or presentation, so in this chapter we will focus on how appealing to ethics and logic will make you an amazing presenter.

An emotional appeal by itself may not be enough

to make someone listen to you – people fixate on different aspects based on their experience and personality. So involving ethics and logic can only help you.

Ethos

Ethos means ethics, which in our context is more closely related to your reputation as a speaker.

As mentioned, people are constantly covertly asking themselves "Why should I care?" when engaging in activities or listening to people. One of the most effective answers to this question is "Because I'm an expert."

Ethos is all about appealing to expertise, authority, and reputation. Your audience is more receptive because you are trustworthy, familiar, and in a position of legitimate authority.

Using ethos gets an audience on your side because you are appealing to their need for external validation and expertise. Let's face it – lots of people represent things about themselves that are plainly false or stretched to the limit. People are always trying to persuade us of something, but how do we know whom to trust and believe?

That's where ethos becomes important. If you can

show you have a reputation of expertise and knowledge, people will automatically listen to you and lower their guards for you.

How can you appeal to ethos in your presentation or performance?

First, be certain to mention your education, publications, or any awards you've received in your area of expertise – and any institutions with which you are associated. These are objective markers of expertise and knowledge, and you're essentially borrowing their credibility.

Second, show up early to welcome your audience or connect with them in other ways off the stage. Reputation can be built simply by engaging with your audience firsthand and making sure that you demonstrate your trustworthiness and knowledge to them. Reputation is sometimes built off of assumptions and second or third-hand observations.

If you can greet someone warmly, remind them who you are, and talk a little bit about your qualifications, it's all too easy to make a new fan. You need to show them your human side, not just the side of you that appears intimidating on stage.

Third, tell stories that highlight your ethics. Since

credibility is the key to any ethos-based appeal, tell stories about how trustworthy or knowledgeable you are on a topic. Tell stories that put people's fear that you are a lying scammer at ease, and emphasize traits such as integrity, trustworthiness, morality, kindness, generousness, and intelligence.

People usually rely on small external cues and triggers to determine how they feel about others. Most people are consciously unaware they do this, but they are always looking for people to trust. Once you highlight your traits, they'll run with that one external cue and cast you in a positive light.

Aside from stories that highlight your ethics, you should use stories to highlight your potential similarity to an audience. Very few people see themselves as unreliable and of ill repute, so if you can cast yourself in a similar light to your audience, you will almost automatically gain their trust and validation.

Finally, to increase your reputation and legitimacy, use statistics and references from objective sources – but make sure the sources are ones the audience considers legitimate and respects. This instantly makes you credible because you've spoken to your audience on their level with the necessary backup, and shown that you understand their context.

Would you be more swayed at a cat conference by someone who cited the work of the most current and innovative cat researchers, or someone who cited the work of dog researchers and older cat researchers? That's a pithy, but illustrative, example.

Logos

As mentioned earlier, you can work an audience by either appealing to their emotions, ethics, or sense of logic. With logos, you are appealing to their sense of objective reason and critical thinking.

Everybody has critical thinking skills, and by using a logos based appeal, you make people draw logical conclusions about your value and knowledge. When you make clear arguments with clear conclusions, trust is built between you and the audience.

If your arguments are sound and valid, you are a trustworthy expert: if A and B are true, then it certainly must stand to reason that C is true, where C is your expertise.

How can you incorporate logos into your

presentation or speech?

First, to be logically sound, you must make sure your concepts or theses flow logically.

Don't make leaps of faith based on faulty or nonexistent assumptions, and don't suddenly go from A to Z without explaining what's involved between the two. What you're saying must logically flow easily and stand up to scrutiny. It must be realistic and not require the audience to suspend their disbelief. The audience members must be able to look at your reasoning and admit, "I see how that makes sense."

Second, use plain language.

Whenever people use a fancy word in place of a simple word, it almost always appears as if they are attempting to look smart. It's a red flag to people that you may be trying to conceal a gap in your logic. You get the same effect when you use 100 words to explain a concept, peppering in buzzwords, when the same concept is better explained in 10 words. You have to respect people's intelligence if you're going to be using a logic based approach with your audience.

Third, use diagrams and visuals.

As the old saying goes, "A picture is worth a thousand words." An appeal to logic is best supported with a concrete visual depiction, especially if the logic goes through many steps. Visuals allow you to explain each step, connect them, and irrefutably make them flow right before their eyes.

Fourth, logos based appeals are naturally very heavy on citable findings and statistics. Back up your assertions. I hope this part is self-explanatory.

Finally, address the greatest flaw in your argument or concept, and then refute it.

There are always two sides to any story, so make sure that you present the opposition's argument against you. You have to do this in an intellectually honest way, so you can't present their weakest argument and downplay their positive one. You will look self-aware and logical when you acknowledge that your argument or proposition has weaknesses or flaws.

After you've done that you can proactively attack those arguments on your own terms, instead of being reactionary and defensive. When you bring up your opposition's greatest argument and refute it, you are controlling the story and addressing it in the exact way that you want to skew it.

Logic is making the best decision at the time with the information presented, so it behooves you to present all of the information on your terms.

Chapter 12. Visualize, Rehearse, and Memorize

Every single high performer does it. Your favorite athlete does it. Your favorite actor or actress probably does it too.

You've probably also done it from time to time. Have you ever closed your eyes and walked around your house trying to visualize where you left your keys?

Visualization is a powerful rehearsal technique that is underrated by most, and written off as too placebo-esque and abstract by others.

There is more to visualization than looking at yourself in the mirror and saying, "I can do this because I am the world's champion!"

Effective visualization is when you mentally rehearse all the steps required to achieve a goal – every single minute step. The value is in exercising your mental pathways before you actually do something, which makes you catch mistakes and inconsistencies you would otherwise make. And it allows you to think more critically about what you want to accomplish, and how.

When you visualize success you create the concrete framework for that vision.

Before going into detail about what the two types of effective visualization really look like, I want to talk a little more about how visualizing your successful outcome can make your rehearsal substantially more effective.

First, visualizing encompasses every step from beginning to end, including the eventual successful conclusion.

When you visualize every step, you will realize what steps you have been missing, which steps require more thought and need to be altered, and what steps will lead to shortcuts you should explore.

In other words, visualization allows you to creatively and objectively analyze the best path to success before you even hit the stage. If you don't visualize, you won't have the freedom to brainstorm creatively because you won't feel free to take risks. When you visualize, you can throw out and toss around all kinds of possibilities you otherwise wouldn't because there is no cost (or real risk) to the process – except for some possible mental strain.

The steps involved in visualization can be done from the comfort of your bed in a matter of minutes.

In a sense, visualizing enables you to "wing it" far more easily. If you visualize effectively and often, you won't need to physically rehearse an action or performance beforehand. The work will all be mental, and for all intents and purposes, your second or third run through can be close to a final product.

Last but not least, visualization can make your rehearsal more effective by breaking it into small, individual steps that you can tackle one by one. It's very intimidating to look at a task, a path to success, or a big accomplishment as impossible to achieve from the outset. One, huge insurmountable task before you can be stymieing, whereas its parts, approached singly, can be very easy to manage.

Remember, every achievement is made up of a number of smaller achievements, and it's encouraging and confidence building to break your success down into a number, even a large number, of simpler steps. This can mean the difference between eagerly beginning a task, or dragging your feet kicking and screaming into a task because you imagine it to be so huge and painful.

As I alluded to before, there are two main ways of mentally rehearsing and visualizing your outcome for greater chances of success. They both involve pretending you are sitting in a dark movie theater and you are watching a movie in which you are the main character.

There are two movies and you are doing one of two things:

The first movie is from a *first-person perspective* and you are going through every step required to achieve something. Examine every nuance, and perform every little part. Place yourself in that situation emotionally and mentally. It is like rehearsing and preparing ahead of time for the stress and curveballs to come. For example, a kicker on a football team might watch himself get called from the sideline, be jeered by opposing fans, and set up his kick perfectly.

The second movie you will watch is one in which you perform an action perfectly from a *third-person perspective*. This allows you to focus on the technical steps involved and remember the feeling of doing it correctly. You'll pick up on small things that you wouldn't if you hadn't mentally rehearsed it beforehand. Here, the football kicker might replay kicking the ball and nailing the field goal over and over, counting the number of steps, the angle at which he kicks, and how much strength he gives it.

Mental rehearsal positions your success as inevitability.

Visualization has many logical and commonsense benefits and is supported by science.

French scientists believe that it doesn't matter whether we are only imagining actions, or actually doing them in the real world. The brain doesn't differentiate between the two very much, which means that the same neural connections and networks are created and used in either case. It's as if you are blazing a trail for your neural connections before they need to be used in real life.

The implications of this are that mental practice is as physical practice. Indeed, a 2007 study showed that athletes who mentally rehearsed one particular exercise had the exact same strength gains as athletes who actually did the exercise physically.

Visualization can be extremely powerful and is a severely underrated success technique.

Now what about rehearsal that is specific to presentations and performances? Performances present their own unique challenges.

First, when you rehearse your presentation or speech, don't always start from the beginning. When you do this, you usually end up just doing the same part over and over, sleepwalking through the middle portions, and then waking up at the ending. You may be mastering the beginning and ending, but not the middle 50% of your speech.

So start at a point that is 25%, 50%, and 75% into your talk. Ever hear that term "knowing something forwards and backwards"? This is how you reach that point of mastery. You should be able to start cold from any of these points, which will make you a far better presenter.

Second, being on stage presents some unique challenges. You'll have extremely bright lights focused on your face, and people often underestimate how blinding they are. They can literally be blinding and hurt your retinas to look at, so this is an important factor to account for when you rehearse.

The lights can also generate a lot of heat, so being ready for heat and sweat is a good idea.

You may or may not be used to holding a microphone, so you'll have to modulate your behavior to make sure one of your hands is always occupied. Does the microphone have a cord? Then you also need to be aware of where the cord lies and not trip over it.

Third, a cardinal sin when you're on stage is facing away from the audience. Make sure your natural mannerisms when pacing or turning always keep you facing the audience.

Finally, don't wait for your postmortem dissection to practice in front of a mirror or record yourself either with video or audio.

When you combine all these elements, your rehearsal might look a little comical. You'll have a few lamps pointing directly at you, you'll be wearing a warm coat regardless of the weather, and you'll be speaking into a water bottle meant to represent a microphone. On top of that, you'll be recording it all! You might look ridiculous in rehearsal, but rehearsing for the worst of conditions while hoping for the best is great preparation. Imagine how easy your performance will be if you've already put yourself through a worst case scenario and none of those factors bother you!

All of your visualization and rehearsal will be for naught if you don't memorize your material. As with so many things, thousands of years ago the ancient Greeks came up with a way to accomplish this – they called it the method of loci, and in modern days, it's known as the memory palace technique.

Proven through thousands of years of practice, and not coincidentally also the main tactic used by most memory contest champions, the memory palace hijacks additional parts of the brain that aren't typically used for memorization to aid in its task. When you build a memory palace you are harnessing your spatial brain capacity.

Here's the easiest, lowest-resistance way to build your memory palace to aid in memorizing your presentation.

First, visualize your apartment or house.

Walk through it in your mind. This will be your memory palace. Decide on a route that you will take when you enter, such as going to the kitchen, your bedroom, then sitting on your couch. This route must not change.

Second, identify specific items along your route as "storage locations" – this is where you'll be placing memories to pick up later.

For example, in your kitchen you have a (1) refrigerator and (2) stove; in your bedroom you have (3) a red pillow and (4) a green rug; and on your couch you can see your (5) television and (6) bobblehead collection. Those are six distinct items you can recall just by visualizing your home!

Third, now we assign things we want to memorize to those six items along the path in your memory palace. For example, put a big neon billboard on each of the six distinct items in your memory palace that I described, noting what you want to remember. It might be six different parts of your speech, or three parts of your opening and three parts of your closing.

Fourth, be creative and vivid. Use symbols, drawings, or other concepts that are associated with what you want to remember.

For example, say my memory palace is designed to remember four things: car brands. The objects in my physical home I use are my couch, refrigerator, flower vase, and shoe rack.

Instead of just affixing a label to each, I would put something vivid that would make me remember the car brand. On the couch, I would put a picture of Hitler to remember Volkswagen, a German car brand. On the refrigerator, I would put a picture of a Samurai to evoke Honda, a Japanese car brand. On the flower vase, I would put a picture of James Bond to make me think of the Aston Martin, which is his trademark car he drives in most of the eponymous movies.

Finally, walk through your memory palace! Take your normal route through the palace and remember how many objects there are in each location. When you take the normal route, you'll inevitably encounter your six storage locations so you can then use the vivid imagery you've placed along the route to evoke whatever you wanted to memorize.

Chapter 13. Create Pre-performance Rituals

Before I step onto any stage for a speech, performance, or even before I have an important phone call, I have a ritual.

I try not to talk to anyone for at least fifteen minutes beforehand, I don't eat for at least an hour beforehand, I do my vocal warm up exercises, three sets of pushups, and even if it's a phone call I dress myself as if it's an in-person meeting. I don't listen to music, I pace, and I go to the bathroom at the last possible moment before I hit the stage. It's a relatively simple ritual.

A ritual is simply something that gets you into game mode. It prepares you mentally and physically, and occasionally emotionally. It can encompass anything, is different for everyone, and all high performers do it. Kind of sounds like a riddle, doesn't it?

Creating your pre-performance ritual is about identifying your optimal state for performance, and making sure that you can reach that point mentally every time you need it. Everyone is different, so it's important to take note of how you feel to find out your optimal state.

It's a matter of asking yourself the right questions.

For instance, do you warm up better by being social before you speak in public, or do you need time alone to go over your notes? How long does your ritual need to be to adequately deliver any benefit? Do you like to speak or perform on a full or empty stomach? Do you get nervous and need to walk off the adrenaline?

Whatever you do physically often has an internal effect. Just as our internal reality impacts our external behavior, our external behavior can have a strong effect on how we feel inside.

This ritual has to be personal. It has to be completely about you. Following someone else's ritual doesn't mean you will get the same results. What follows are a few typical aspects of a pre-performance ritual that you can consider when creating your own.

Your Food

Pay attention to what you eat. What makes you burp, what makes you feel sluggish, and what makes you feel ready? Does eating make you hiccup, for example?

Pay attention to quantity, timing beforehand, what you eat, and how much water you need to you keep yourself hydrated (but not so much that you feel like you have to run to the bathroom mid-speech!).

Do certain foods constantly get stuck in your teeth, or make you produce phlegm in your throat?

Is eating relaxing for you and will it make your performance feel like just a normal part of your day? Does eating put you in a good mood? Does your stomach make noises if you eat too much, or too little?

I don't recommend going on stage with an empty stomach; that can actually make you light-headed in some circumstances. Personally I like to eat a light meal with plenty of fluids about an hour before a performance. That way, it doesn't matter what or how much I eat because there is time to wake up or brush my teeth.

Prepare your digestive system for optimal performance too.

Your Activity

Activity includes napping and physical activity designed to warm you up or otherwise burn off excess adrenaline that might cause your voice or hands to shake.

If your performance is later in the day, would you feel more refreshed if you took a nap sometime during that day? Would you feel too groggy? Or would you even worry that you wouldn't wake up in time?

Some people take brisk walks or, like me, do pushups to focus themselves, warm up their bodies, and work off the nervous energy that comes when you're excited about something.

Some people don't like to move at all, and instead will sequester themselves in a corner of a room and sit with their thoughts in solitude.

Your Superstitions

I don't have any, but plenty of people do. These people may not even believe in superstitions per se, but if something makes them feel better and more confident at game time, then there's no reason to discourage it.

Some people like to wear certain clothes they think are lucky. Other people have lucky charms. Sometimes speakers brush their hair or do some other specific physical act they think will increase their likelihood of success.

It's a self-creating cycle because once you associate success with a certain object or action you attempt to catch lightning in a bottle by recreating the exact conditions that existed for a prior success.

Superstitions probably don't have any real power in and of themselves, but they get your mind in the right place and set you at ease. 50% of success is believing you will have success, and that is their real power.

Your Social Interaction

Does being around others warm you up and make you perform optimally? Or do you need to hide from others to preserve your energy and go over last minute thoughts?

Pay attention to your social patterns and what tends to stress you out or calm you down. Perhaps being around strangers causes unnecessary anxiety, but being around your significant other has a calming effect.

We all have a finite amount of willpower and energy for each day. Are you wasting yours, or priming yourself for "the zone" when you speak to others before a performance?

In a similar vein, maybe there is a song that puts you in the right mood that you can use to instead of people before a performance. It can be a song to relax and soothe you, or pump your energy up and get your heartbeat dancing.

Whatever the case, people or the lack thereof can affect you emotionally and distract you – make sure that you figure out which combination makes you feel positive, energized, and empowered before your performance.

Your Rehearsal

How much will you rehearse your performance beforehand? Do you feel the need to run through it until the last possible moment, or do you prefer to clear your mind and rely on your hours of visualization and rehearsal?

Will you skim everything once, say the entire speech out loud to yourself, or feverishly look through index cards?

Think about what you did before a big test when you were in school. How did you prefer to maximize your opportunity? Would you cram until the last minute, or use those moments to clear your mind and handle the pending stress?

The bottom line about pre-performance rituals is simple. When you prepare yourself physically, your brain takes note and follows. The human brain prefers to see patterns, so if you give it a pattern in the form of your routine, you can more easily guarantee an optimal performance. Never ever overlook the power of ritual.

The pre-performance rituals of some famous performers may surprise you. For example, standup comic Louie CK's routine is decidedly anti-social and introspective.

He doesn't listen to the radio or music on the way to his show; he uses that time to think about his act. After he arrives at the venue, he generally just sits in silence until his turn. He actively avoids talking to people, but sometimes observes the audience's reaction to other comics so he knows what he's going to be facing. Once the spotlight hits him, he turns the knob all to way to 11.

The singer Lorde has a fairly interesting pre-performance ritual as well. She eats certain foods such as seaweed or berries as her dinner before a performance. Then she takes a short nap with her favorite blanket. Finally, she wears one special outfit that she wears to all her performances. This gives her a tremendous sense of ease, comfort, and confidence. She has said, "Once I've got my suit on, I can do anything."

Just pay attention to what actions set you at ease and get your mind in the right place.

Chapter 14. Close on a High Note

Some people debate ad nauseum as to whether the opening or the closing of a presentation or performance is more important.

The answer? It doesn't matter. Both are equally important – remember the primary and recency effects I talked about earlier?

The surprising part to most people is that openings and closings can also contain many of the same elements. Why wouldn't something that is attention grabbing work great at both the beginning and the end?

Closings carry the responsibility of summarizing

and making sure that matters are wrapped up with a neat bow. If at the end of your speech you cannot tie in the main points you raised in the beginning, it's easy for your speech to fall flat. If you are lost about what the purpose of your speech even was, how do you think your audience members will feel?

So your closing has two duties: it must answer the question, "What was the main purpose of the speech?" and it must be memorable and catchy. Combine both, marinate, and serve with wit and humor.

Catchphrase

Remember your catchphrase? The one that encompassed everything your presentation was about in one sentence? You've probably said it a few times throughout your speech, but you can't neglect to use it in your closing.

This is when you circle back to it, repeat it, and break down for the final time what it means on a macro level. When you use your catchphrase and an ensuing explanation as your closing, it ties everything together and reinforces the main purpose of your speech.

For example, "The more we move, the less we die

(the catchphrase – morbid, I know). There is indisputable evidence from scientists that sitting is a gateway that prevents us from happiness (main argument 1). Main argument 2. Main argument 3. The more we move, the less we die. Thank you."

Mirror Your Introduction

Use whatever tactic you used at the beginning for your opener when you close.

If you used a rhetorical question, you might ask it again and answer it differently in light of the new knowledge the audience has. "So I ask you again, do you love your grandparents? Based on what I've talked about, it may not matter…"

If you used a shocking statistic, you might repeat it and touch on how you explained the phenomena behind it. "Remember when I said that 1 out of every 5 people who swim in the ocean die from shark attacks? Well, now we know that it's a skewed statistic because…"

If you used a personal anecdote, you might refer to it again and talk about how you would have acted differently with the knowledge you've given the audience. "Yes, I was a fat kid. But had I known what I've told you today…"

There is something very psychologically satisfying about closing by coming full circle and mirroring your introduction. It brings a sense of satisfaction and introduces the same information in a different context, which can have a powerful and impactful effect.

Callback

A callback, as explained earlier in the book, is when you integrate elements of a prior topic or joke into the current topic or joke.

A callback, however, should be carefully chosen because of its importance. When you callback as a closing, use an emotional high point or particularly funny moment. For example, if people clapped loudly, cheered, or laughed, refer to one of those points again.

The key here is to get people to remember the value they found in your speech and capitalize on the emotions you invoked before. The audience could have been clapping about a central theme, a big joke, or some sort of catchphrase that you used. Whatever the case, you need to bring it back to their attention so they will remember and appreciate your speech overall.

"So, yes, even though I tripped on my supervisor's

rug that day, I still learned something about leadership."

Personal Anecdote

Of course, this is a different personal anecdote from the one you may have used in your opener. But it's an anecdote that still relates to the main purpose of your presentation.

Draw people into your world and make them viscerally feel your purpose. Connect emotionally and make them relate.

What kind of anecdote should you use, if you use a different one at the closing?

You can use a before-and-after method, where the prior anecdote was about your experience before you had the knowledge you've spoken about, and your closing anecdote is one that demonstrates how different life is after having that knowledge.

For example, "After I learned how to successfully balance my checkbook and budget, I went to Hawaii on my first vacation in years. It was amazing…"

Invoke the Consequences

Invoking the consequences is when you highlight all the negative things that will happen if the audience fails to take heed or action.

When you call the crowd to action, it tells them that there was a point to what you said. There was a good reason they showed up to listen to you speak. You have to call people to action, otherwise it's too easy for people to walk away thinking, "What was the point of all that?"

One of the best ways to call people to action is to talk about what will happen if they don't act on your suggestions. If they don't follow through on your call to action, what consequences will come about?

This has to be very visceral and painful. You basically have to ask the question, "How bad could it get?" and describe exactly how bad it will get.

You must highlight the negative consequences and then play up the positive effects of their taking action.

For example, "There's no way around it. If you don't take action, the whaling industry will destroy the entire ecosystem. Wildlife, fish, entire industries will fall into ruin just because some people like the way whale blubber burns as oil.

After the industries fail..."

Direct Call to Action

Politicians do this constantly, and it's not unlike the prior technique of invoking the consequences. It's often a rhetorical question, or part of one.

For example, "Are you ready to support me and become a part of the solution for our great country?"

"You can't not act now that you have this knowledge. I want you to go home, write a letter to your congressman, and send it immediately. Don't sit idly by as our wildlife suffers for our vanity."

"You know what you need to do! I want you to take out your phone right now, put this number in, and save it. When you get outside to the parking lot, call it, and tell them you want your money back!"

Closing on a high note should be an easy task if you have made it to this point of the book!

Chapter 15. Manhandling the Q&A

There may not be exact statistics to prove it, but it seems that no matter what kind of presentation you give, there is almost always a question and answer (Q&A) session afterward. Many organizers may even cut generously into your actual presentation time in favor of a longer Q&A session.

What does this mean for you? A couple of things.

First, you might think your job is done and you're scot-free after you get through your presentation. Not so.

The more important or complex your presentation

is, the less true this will be. If you're presenting in front of twenty people about the benefits of exercise, you probably won't get too many questions. But if you're presenting in front of 2,000 people about the benefits of specific types of cardiovascular exercise on your lung capacity, your work is only half done after you present.

Second, prepare to be cut short and interrupted. There are bound to be more complex parts of your presentation that, despite your best efforts, will confuse people. You can ask for people to save their questions til the end, but you may not be able to control your time constraints or people's hand-raising impulses.

During your presentation or speech, you're completely in control of what you're going to talk about: when, how, and why. It's a script that *you* have executive control over. A Q&A session is more like a minefield because you literally have no idea what will be asked or brought up – and it's a good bet that people will ask about details, opposing views, and skepticism.

Given their unpredictable nature and how prevalent Q&A sessions are, you should allocate more than just a passing moment to prepare for it.

Don't allow yourself to lose credibility by getting

blindsided by a question you didn't anticipate.

Common Questions Sheet

If you're well-versed in a topic (and presumably you are because you are speaking about it), you'll know the common concerns, questions, opposing arguments, and studies regarding it.

For example, if you're making an argument based on a study, you should also know the two studies that contradict your study but are flawed. It's your business to know about your topic.

The first tip in handling the Q&A is to create a "Common questions sheet" that makes note of the common arguments against your position, and the clarifications you'll need to make. This is the single-most valuable piece of advice in handling your Q&A session. By thinking carefully about likely questions ahead of time, and generating answers to them so you don't have to think on the fly will make a huge difference in how polished you appear.

Your list might turn out to be longer than you think, but by making the list and going over it, you'll be able to fill in your knowledge gaps by addressing each common question in detail.

Repeat the Question for Clarity

Repeating the question has two purposes. First, it allows the audience to clearly hear the question.

Second, when you repeat and restate the question, you give the asker a chance to clarify the meaning and intent behind their question. They might not be articulate or well-informed enough to know exactly what to ask, so if you repeat their question and even rephrase it, you can put it into the proper context and make sure that you are answering what they are asking.

For example, an audience member asks "What are the implications of daily usage of this substance?"

You may need to repeat their question, "Well, the study did mention the implications of daily usage, but to clarify, are you asking about the effects of the particular protein involved in the substance? Is that what you meant?"

Other times, you might need to ask them to rephrase their question to make sense of it.

Don't Answer Questions Literally

When friends or acquaintances ask you about your weekend, they don't actually care. They just want to hear something interesting, and often answering literally about your weekend is not very interesting. You should treat Q&A questions the same – don't answer them literally.

When somebody asks you a short question, don't just pop back with an equally short answer.

Many questions can be answered with a simple yes or no, but if you do that the audience members might not fully get what you're saying. The better approach is to go into the background of the answer. You're trying to impart a thorough understanding, and that doesn't happen with a yes or no answer.

Here's a good method for tackling short, or seemingly unrelated questions: give a short answer, then a long answer.

For example, you may get asked "Is it safe to drive at night after that type of eye surgery?"

You would answer "Well, the short answer is yes, it is. Now let's dive a bit into the background of why that is..."

Stop to Think

Seriously. You might not think this is necessary to

say, but experience has proven otherwise.

Pause for a few seconds, gather your thoughts, and then proceed with your answer. Don't be afraid of the momentary silence your thought gathering creates.

The reason you want to stop and think before you answer is so you don't automatically answer questions based on reflex.

Give yourself time to wrap your mind completely around the question and try to ascertain if there is anything below the surface level of the question you should address. Make sure you haven't misunderstood them.

Analyze what the question is, what it leads to, and what ulterior motives or agendas are behind the question.

This can go a long way in bulletproofing your answers, or at least ensuring that you don't paint yourself into a corner. The real challenge is in doing all of this in only a few seconds!

Frame Your Answer with Your Audience in Mind

You always have to remember your audience and what the purpose of your speech was. They showed up for a specific reason, so try to avoid rambling on tangents or indulging audience members who want to ask about unrelated things. Offer to speak about those unrelated questions after the formal Q&A session.

There's a fixed sphere of knowledge they are interested in. Stay focused on them.
Consider the probability of values being created or lost when you answer a particular question. If it's obvious that most people in the audience really don't care about the specific question asked, it's safe to tell that person you will answer it later.

Get Personal

Getting personal consists of two main things for a Q&A session. First, ask for their name, and tell them it's nice to meet them.

Second, make eye contact with the asker.

Just like the rest of your presentation, try to inject a conversational feel and tone into the Q&A session. This means addressing the audience member as an individual and speaking to them directly. It makes people feel special and as if they matter.

Break Down Long Questions

When some people ask a question, they tend to arrive at their question only after thinking out loud for some time. This often results in a confusing, long, or multi-part question.

It's tempting to disregard people like this or ask them to rephrase, but there's another effective technique you can use to your advantage – creating your own group of questions.

It's deceptively simple. Upon hearing a garbled string of gibberish, reply with "Well, I hear you. It sounds as if you're asking a few questions about the manufacturing process, first about the location, second about the efficacy, and third about wages. I'll answer them all in turn..."

Break long, complex questions into simpler, shorter ones of your own choosing. More often than not, you're answering what they are actually asking, and your ability to simplify and clarify the question makes you appear insightful and intuitive.

Give a Half Answer

A half answer isn't an incomplete answer; it's merely an answer to just one part of the question that's been asked.

You can tell an audience member, "In the interest of saving time, let me just answer one part of your question."

If you feel you have to clarify that you're not being evasive or crafty, you can also say, "Given that I've already answered other parts of your question, let me address this one particular part."

Finally, you may just be more interested in talking about one part of the question, in which case you can say "Now the second part of your question is really something that's interesting to address and think about..."

Turn the Tables

Finally, if there are fewer questions than you expected, turn the tables on the audience and ask them for feedback on particularly controversial, interesting, or illuminating parts.

For example, "I'd love to hear any thoughts or feedback you have on just how wide the gap we discovered between mammals and primates is. It was incredibly shocking to everyone involved in the study."

Audience members may not be shy, but they are

often afraid of judgment. You may be able to tease out more questions and discussion by directing specific questions and statements toward them. There is far less judgment in answering a question as opposed to asking one.

Chapter 16. Postmortem Analysis

Like most people, I hate watching myself on video or even hearing a recording of my voice.

Back when I was in college, I performed on stage quite a bit as part of music groups and bands. When it came to our weekly review, the first thing we did was pull up a video of our most recent performance for constructive feedback for everyone in the group.

I've never cringed more in my life than the first few times we did this, but it made a huge difference in our overall stage presence and performance skills. We are all our own worst critics, and sometimes that works to our advantage.

Becoming an ace on stage is a process that involves a learning curve. Nothing will be perfect the first time you try it, but the length of that learning curve depends on you.

The only constant should be continuous evolution and learning. Always be on the lookout for how you can improve your game. Even the most polished public speaker can use some improvement.

The best way to do this is to record your performances and perform objective and detached postmortems on them. Think of a postmortem like grading a test, where the performance was the test. It's only fair and smart to evaluate your performance to see where you can improve, what your weaknesses are, and how to overall utilize your experience.

Most of the things you'll be paying attention to during your postmortem won't be about the material itself. They'll be about your presentation and presence.

The best way to glean insight about your material is to record the Q&A session and then debrief that portion of your presentation. You're looking to see if the same questions, clarifications, or arguments come up frequently. If they do, the evidence is plain that these are concepts or areas you need to improve with additional clarification or by dedicating more time to them.

The Audience is a Barometer

The audience is always giving off signals that you can learn from. It's up to you whether you want to pay attention and take advantage of these signals and learn from them.

One of the first things to observe during your postmortem is how the audience reacts to your jokes, explanations, and stories. When did people clap, when did they laugh, and when was there awkward silence because of a bad joke or pun? Could you hear the audience talking among themselves at technical points, or could you hear gasps and shocked awe when you unveiled a particularly effective visual?

How much and when was the audience speaking among themselves? This usually indicates boredom. So where in your presentation was your audience captive, and when were they bored enough to chatter?

During your postmortem you will also be able to

gauge which topics your audience reacted to most, and which they didn't react to at all. These observations should inform your future decisions.

Speech Rate

Recall that for most people, their rate of speech during a presentation or performance is way too fast. For some, it borders on unintelligible, and sometimes we don't even realize it until we are struggling for breath.

Are you speaking so fast that you cloud your clarity or enunciation? Are you speaking so rapidly that you lose all inflection and emotion in your voice? Are there pauses where there should be pauses, or do you appear to be opposed to commas?

Remember that a fast rate of speech is the single biggest flag for nervousness.

Fidgeting and Overall Body Language

Are you somewhere between being a statue and an inflatable balloon man in terms of movement? Do you keep rubbing your face or nose, or touching your glasses?

Are you shifting your weight from side to side as if you have to visit the restroom? Are your gestures done at a moderate pace and not manic?

Are you fidgeting? Do you have some facial tics, some sort of speech tics, or quirks? How can you minimize them or, better yet, how can you use them to your advantage?

Finally, is your overall body language defensive and closed-off, or is it open and confident with your chin up and chest out?

Check Your Emotions

Your emotions will be conveyed to the audience verbally and non-verbally. Are your emotions coming through loud and clear in each medium?

Verbally, are you using enough vocal inflection to convey feeling, especially within a story? Non-verbally, is it possible to tell the emotion you are trying to convey if you put yourself on mute? Your facial expressions are paramount to this.

Is there consistency in both cases? Or does one contradict or lessen the power of the other?

Reading from Notes

To what extent are you relying on your notes and visuals, as opposed to using them to accentuate certain points? It's important to be essentially off-note for maximum effect, as you can see in standup comics. That's when you can read an audience and tailor your performance on the fly, like calling an audible at the line of scrimmage in a football game.

If you're not reading from your notes, where are you looking? Are you making a comfortable amount of eye contact with audience members in different sectors?

Energy Level

As I've mentioned, your energy level should be just one to two notches above that of the audience. Are you keeping it that high, or are there times when your energy level hits a lull? Are there patterns in the fluctuations of your energy levels?

Are you coming out of the gates hot and high and you are closing on a high point?

Is your energy level consistently high and modulated for effect during stories?

Words or Phrases You Stumble Over

Some phrases are just difficult to say out loud. We don't notice it when we write them in our notes or choose our vocabulary, but… *Sometimes Six Sick Speakers Say Stupid Statements on Route to Unique New York*. You'll never realize that you can't easily or properly pronounce or enunciate some words or phrases until you crash and burn trying them out in front of an audience for the first time.

It's never an isolated word; it's a word accompanied by other words in a phrase. Watch your recording and ruthlessly prune out words you fumble and stumble over and replace them with simpler words. Your presentation shouldn't be a recreation of an Ernest Hemingway novel – people aren't coming for your effusive vocabulary and verbal prose. Just deliver your message and they will be more than happy.

Eliminate Filler Words and Phrases

You're probably very familiar with filler words and phrases: um, uh, you know, I mean, and like.

The reason these pop up is because people are uncomfortable with even a second of silence in their presentation. So while they are thinking about their response or their next topic, they use a filler word to eliminate that silence.

First of all, pauses are a natural part of

conversation and dialogue, and for an audience to never hear one is a bit uncomfortable (and weird). Give yourself room to breathe and give the audience a break as well.

Second, if your speech is properly written and rehearsed in advance, there should be little reason for filler words and phrases. Talk out loud when fleshing out your concepts so you can write a fuller outline of your material.

Third, you can observe where you use filler words and phrases the most – it's probably during a section with which you are the least comfortable or about which you have the weakest grasp. If I were to ask you to explain to me how to tie a shoelace, there wouldn't be any filler words or phrases because you know the procedure so well. The converse is true when you lack knowledge.

Finally, literally count your filler words. Tally them up and look at the visual representation of how much comfortable silence you prevent. Hopefully this will make a tangible impact on your delivery.

Chapter 17. Easy, Quick, and Actionable

If you're looking for a few quick wins and upgrades to your speech and presentation skills, this chapter addresses some easy and actionable tips.

Visuals and Props

Visuals are helpful and props are even better.

Props tell people that there are real-world implications for what you're saying. They will fixate on it. They see in 3D form the material manifestation of the concepts you're talking about in your speech. Of course you shouldn't go overboard. You shouldn't rely too heavily on props for each and every point of your speech. That's overkill and will dilute the overall force and power of your speech.

The best kind of prop is subtle but related to your overall point.

Speak as if You are Talking to One Person

Many speakers have a tough time talking to a crowd because they address the whole crowd. Their speech becomes overly formal and they speak unnaturally, which robs them of any natural charm they have.

In their minds, they are dealing with a huge number of people and it can get quite intimidating on both sides.

Speak as if you are talking to a close friend, one to one. The casual tone and confidence you'll project will create comfort on both sides of the stage and make your audience more receptive to your presentation overall.

Watch the Masters

There are many famous speakers. It would behoove you to do some homework by watching them and taking notes.

They don't have to be politicians or CEOs of large corporations; they can simply be great at connecting with audiences or conveying ideas. Master speakers take many shapes and forms.

Predictably, a group I recommend paying attention to is standup comics. Their entire job is to win over an audience and evoke emotions, so it's safe to say they're effective.

After you've watched a wide variety of speakers, you'll come away with a good sense of the kind of presenter you want to be. You should be able to point to someone's delivery and stage presence as an end goal for yourself – in fact, make it a point to name three role models in this context. See which of their strengths you can take for yourself and integrate into your own individual style.

Don't Overcorrect

It's easy to spot an error in what you're saying and correct it in real time.

But when you do this, it's easy to stumble over your errors and your correction of errors, which creates even more errors. Imagine saying that sentence aloud on stage, and you'll get a sense of what you should avoid in overcorrecting. It also has the tendency to make you look unconfident, unsure, and consequently untrustworthy.

And whatever you do, don't apologize for verbal flubs or draw additional attention to them. The audience has already noticed and probably doesn't care. When you apologize, it only makes it seem as if you are self-conscious about it.

Don't get too preoccupied regarding your errors. It happens to the best of us. Just move on.

Don't Take Yourself Too Seriously

This is probably the single best piece of advice I can give.

People don't like others who take themselves too seriously. It's just fact.

Even if your subject matter is serious, you can't take yourself too seriously. This has the opposite effect on what the audience thinks – if you take yourself too seriously, you become incredibly easy to make fun of.

People like to be spoken to in the same casual way a friend speaks to them.

When you take yourself too seriously, this sucks any natural charm you have out of your speech.

You come off unnatural and stiff, which makes you appear inauthentic and not engaging.

Don't be the presentation version of the guy who wears a full suit to work every day despite the fact that everyone else is in sneakers and a t-shirt.

Avoid stiff formality and rigid professionalism – you might think this will garner you respect, but respect doesn't matter if no one wants to spend time with you.

Chapter 18. Don't Be Boring – Guest Chapter by Jason Bax

How many times have you sat through someone's presentation, clinging desperately to the hope that it will get better, but find yourself saying, "Well, that's an hour I'll never get back."?

I passionately believe if you're going to ask someone to give you their undivided attention for anything over 15 minutes, you have a responsibility to deliver *value*; teach them something new, entertain them, or both. Otherwise, you're a thief who's stealing the most precious of commodities from your audience... time.

Here are some of the main principles that have served me well in my speaking career where I regularly steal the show and am remembered for my value.

Nobody Cares About You.

Would you rather watch a list credits at the beginning of a movie or at the end? The end, of course. Why would you care who the directors, costume designers, set decorators, directors of photography, or actors are before you see the movie and decide you care?

It's only at the end of a movie you enjoy that you ask, "I wonder who the actor was who played the villain?"

Unfortunately, you've probably seen speakers that begin their presentations talking about how great they are; from the unicorn species they've rescued from extinction, to the rainforest that was named after her, to the time he gave the Dalai Lama advice on being present.

And the whole time, you were probably thinking to yourself, "When is this windbag going to shut up about themselves and give me what I came for so I can get out of here?"

To put it bluntly, people are selfish and self-centered. To put it delicately, people want to know what's in it for them to listen to your presentation.

If you start your presentation talking about yourself, you're in danger of being painfully boring.

You're putting the movie credits before the movie itself. You first have to give people a reason to want to know you before wasting their time telling them about yourself. Take a cue from Hollywood - don't do it. It's just boring.

So How Should You Start?

Most movies and television shows hook your attention within the first three minutes by starting with an exciting conflict, chase, escape, or explosion. They lead with something that needs to be resolved, solved, or clarified.

What's the inferred and implied promise an action movie makes in the first three minutes? This is going to be an exciting, wild ride!

If you start your presentation like a good Hollywood movie, with excitement or conflict, you'll never bore your audience.

161

How? Here are some ideas you can use.

Conflict.

Take a position that's contrary to common beliefs.

"Most people think X but the truth is Y."

"Most entrepreneurs think you start a business to make money, but the truth is you make the most money when you sell your business."

When you make a statement like this, you're daring your audience to stick around and pay attention so they can see how you resolve the conflict. Make them curious and imply that you have greater and special knowledge.

"Most people think women are attracted to looks or 6-pack abs, but the truth is that women are really attracted to status."

What strong, contrary stance can you state right at the beginning of your talk?

Make a Big, Bold, Ballsy Promise.

"I'm going to show you how to look eight years younger with regular honey in the next 30-

minutes."

"Today, I will show you how to turn your crazy product ideas into money."

"Today, I'm going to show you that pigs really can fly."

If you start your talk with a big, bold, ballsy promise and then deliver on that promise, people will definitely want to know who you are. It creates a sense of mystery that people want resolved. Then you'll have their permission to roll your credits and talk about yourself a bit, without being boring.

Motion Creates Emotion.

Unless you are going to do your best impression of a tree, take Ben Affleck's advice in the movie, *Boiler Room*, "Get off your ass! Move around. Motion creates emotion."

Get out from behind the podium. It's not an anchor or a bunker that will protect you from the mental rotten vegetables people will throw at you if you're boring. Moving around not only stirs up emotion in your body, it adds exciting energy to your voice and gives your audience something more interesting than your slides to stare at.

Work that stage, baby! Walk over and talk to people on the left, the middle, then the right. You may even want to try leaving the safety of the stage and walk into the audience.

Shut Up and Show 'Em.

Who would you rather listen to: (1) a guy talking about the theory of the law of attraction to manifest more money in your life or (2) someone who shows you how he makes real money, live, in real-time, right in front of your eyes?

"I'm going to tell you how to pick up women."

Okay buddy, but why don't you just shut up and show me?

"I'm going to tell you how to get rich."

Great! But first why don't you just log into your bank account and show me how much money you've deposited in the last twelve months, then show me how you did it? Then you'll have my undivided attention.

"I'm going to share the secret of hitting a golf ball 25-yards longer."

Sounds awesome. But I'd rather see it. Why don't you just skip the promise, pick a random audience member, and teach him your "secrets" for longer drives and prove to us that it actually works? Too many people are trying to sell us things that we don't need, so proving that you are who you say you are is a rare luxury.

After watching one too many presentations so painful I begged for someone to stick a fork in my eye, I invested my time synthesizing the elements of a presentation that grabs people by the (eye) balls and makes them want to watch. I call it, *demotainment*. This is the foundation of my stance against being boring. Remember this acronym: **D.E.M.O - T.**

D = Demonstrate.

If a picture is worth a thousand words, a demonstration is worth a million words. If a demonstration is worth a million words, an entertaining demonstration is worth one hundred million words.

Every successful television infomercial is based on a killer demonstration.

What if instead of explaining the specifics of his bulletproof vest, the host were to strap one on himself, pull out his 45-caliber handgun, aim it at his heart, and pull the trigger?

When you're preparing your talk, the first thing you should ask yourself is how you can incorporate a visual demonstration.

E = Entertain.

I think we can agree that on the scale of boring, blenders are pretty high on the list. So instead of talking about how awesome and powerful Blendtec blenders are, shut up and show them by blending the craziest things you can get their hands on, like iPhones, iPads, Star Wars action figures, watches, and so on.

The only reason you've heard of GoPro cameras is because their demo videos of extreme athletes were absolutely awe-inspiring.

How can you skip the boring theory or explanation, and demonstrate your idea using fun, shock or awe?

M = Make It Brief.

In this age of attention scarcity, you have approximately eight seconds to grab attention. If you are able to grab someone's attention, you have about two more minutes to hold their attention before you lose them to something more instantly gratifying like their email inboxes or Facebook.

This relates to the opening scene in action movies concept. Stack the awesome right up front and suck them in.

Respect people's time. Get to the point and let them decide if they want to stick around.

O = Outrageous, Original and/or Over the Top.

A beer mug shaped like a boot is pretty cool but there's only so much you can say about it. That's why the guys at Vat19, a website for curiously awesome products, went over the top and produced an outrageous music video featuring a German model wearing a fur vest, leather pants and a metal studded glasses.

My point is that if someone can come up with an outrageous, original, or over-the-top idea for a beer mug, you can probably come up with a list for your idea. Grab a beer and challenge yourself.

T = Tell Them What To Do Next.

Some people like to be told what to do and others

need to be told what to do.

At the end of every chapter of most self-help books is an action step.

Give them a challenge, a to do list, a list to create, or a website to visit.

Here's an example of "Telling Them What To Do Next":

If you want more crazy examples of people using demotainment to promote themselves or their business, send me an email to demo@jasonbax.com with the subject "demotainment book" or check-out http://www.JasonBax.com.

Don't Read.

Most people suck at reading out loud because it's usually lifeless and wooden.

Imagine how bad movies would be if actors had their noses buried in scripts during a scene. Imagine how badly a standup comic would bomb if he just read jokes off of a page.

If you're going to stand on stage and read your presentation, save your audience the pain of sitting through your narration, and just send the slides and stay home. The audience will thank you.

You may want to write out your presentation word-for-word to feel prepared. That's perfectly acceptable. Print out your presentation, rehearse it and as you memorize it start deleting sentences from your presentation slides until you only have a picture or one word per bullet to jog your memory.

Now, Roll The Credits...

As the spokesman for a tiny, little Canadian tech company, Jason Bax, sold $3.9-Million in 11-months using the speaking and presentation techniques he shared in this chapter. Bax has been invited to speak at the University of Sydney Australia and University of British Columbia's MBA program. He's spent more time on stage on three separate continents than most speakers spend on one.

You may also recognize his face from one of the 75 TV commercials he's been in for Dell, Fisher-Price, Nissan, Campbell's, and Hasbro, among others, as well as the television show *Fringe* or dying a gruesome death in the television show *Supernatural*.

If you want to know more about Bax, Demotainment or his podcast, Self Made - Entrepreneurs Who've Turned Their Ideas Into Dollars (including an interview with Patrick King) you can find him www.jasonbax.com or www.internetmarketing.com.

Conclusion

I suppose I should actually feel thankful for that disastrous presentation on owls I gave in the third grade.

I have a theory that people aren't typically moved to action unless they meet a threshold of discontent or unhappiness. It exists in every avenue of life. Dissatisfied with your job? New job or start your own business.

Standing and sweating nervously in front of that class was enough to push me over the threshold for public speaking skills. It's an incredibly vivid and visceral feeling to be that vulnerable and open for judgment in front of others, even as a third grader.

And I'll say this again: after you acquire public speaking skills, you won't feel vulnerable or judged while you're on stage.

Isn't that great?

Sincerely,

Patrick King
The Social Interaction Specialist
www.PatrickKingConsulting.com

P.S. If you've enjoyed this book, please don't be shy. Drop me a line, leave a review, or both! I love reading feedback, and reviews are the lifeblood of Kindle books, so they are always welcome and greatly appreciated.

Other books by Patrick King include:

CHATTER: Small Talk, Charisma, and How to Talk to Anyone

The Science of Likability: Charm, Wit, Humor, and the 16 Studies That Show You How To Master Them

Speaking and Coaching

Imagine going far beyond the contents of this book and dramatically improving the way you interact with the world and the relationships you'll build.

Are you interested in contacting Patrick for:

- A social skills workshop for your workplace
- Speaking engagements on the power of conversation and charisma
- Personalized social skills and conversation coaching

Patrick speaks around the world to help people improve their lives as a result of the power of building relationships with improved social skills. He is a recognized industry expert, bestselling author, and speaker.

To invite Patrick to speak at your next event or to inquire about coaching, get in touch directly through his website's contact form at http://www.PatrickKingConsulting.com/contact or simply at patrick@patrickkingconsulting.com

Cheat Sheet

Chapter 1. Overcome Anxiety and Stage Fright

Overcoming the anxiety associated with speaking or presenting is a matter of perspective and realizing that people are there to see you. There is also an optimal amount of stress that promotes an optimal performance.

Chapter 2. Nailing Your Opener

Because of the primacy effect, your opener is extremely important. It's your first impression and the audience won't forget it. Keep in mind that your opener begins when you're offstage and being introduced by other people.

Chapter 3. Knowing Your Audience Is Key

If you can successfully discover what motivates your audience, and even why they are there to listen to you, you can more effectively resonate your message with them and be memorable.

Chapter 4. Find Your Core Message and Catchphrase

Work on boiling your value proposition and core message down to a single sentence, and then make it catchy. Repeat this throughout to remind people of your context and make the audience remember you.

Chapter 5. Standup Comics Are Performance Gurus

Standup comics go to war every time they are on stage. They shoot extremely high, and can sink extremely low. Take cues from them and observe how they approach performances.

Chapter 6. How To Make An Emotional Impact

Emotions are what make speakers emotional. You don't remember what people say, but how they make you feel. Detailed stories and speaking with genuine passion are the best ways to emotionally reach people.

Chapter 7. Project Your Emotions

When you're on stage, emotions can be difficult to convey properly. You must exaggerate your verbal and non-verbal emotions to make sure you are seen.

Chapter 8. Rehearse Your Spontaneity

Rehearsed spontaneity makes you far more relatable with the audience because it simulates a conversation as opposed to a lecture.

Chapter 9. The Power Of Stage Presence

Stage presence is the ability to be magnetic on stage and make it so the audience can't take their eyes off of you. Channel aspects of Freddie Mercury and create a stage persona to come out of your shell.

Chapter 10. Always Be Storytelling

Stories, especially personal and vulnerable ones, draw the audience into your world and emphasize whatever point you are trying to make extremely effectively.

Chapter 11. Ethos and Logos

Ethics and logic, respectively. These are ways of increasing your trustworthiness and credibility on stage.

Chapter 12. Visualize, Rehearse, and Memorize

Visualization should have a prominent place in your rehearsal schedule, and for optimal memorization of your presentation, create a memory palace.

Chapter 13. Create Pre-performance Rituals

A pre-performance ritual gets you into the mindset for optimal performance. Everyone functions differently, so it's important to discover what puts you in the right frame of mind.

Chapter 14. Close On A High Note

Your closing is important because of the recency effect. It has the same purpose and effect of the opener, but with the added responsibility of summation.

Chapter 15. Manhandling the Q&A

Start to expect a Q&A session after your presentation – the longer and more formal, the more likely there will be one. The biggest key is to create a "common questions" sheet.

Chapter 16. Postmortem Analysis

A postmortem analysis of your presentation is important to your develop as a speaker. You won't be looking at the material, but rather your presentation, presence, and speaking skills.

Chapter 17. Five Easy, Quick, and Actionable Tips

The five quick and easy tips are to use props or visuals, speak like you're speaking to a single person, watch and learn from masters, don't overcorrect your stumbles and errors, and don't take yourself too seriously.

Chapter 18. Don't Be Boring by Jason Bax

Take a hint from Hollywood and view yourself as demotainment – a speaker who uses demonstrations and entertainment to make their point and become memorable.